T0370934

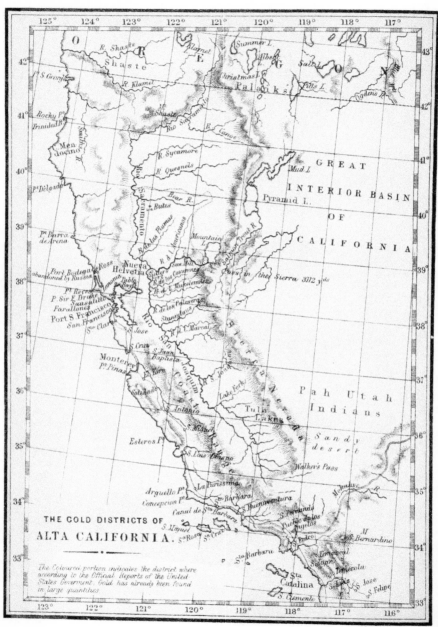

THE GOLD DISTRICTS OF

ALTA CALIFORNIA.

The Coloured portion indicates the district where
according to the Official Reports of the United
States Government, Gold has already been found
in large quantities.

J.R.Jobbins, 3 Warwick Ct.

Published by D. Bogue. 86 Fleet Street.

FOUR MONTHS

AMONG THE GOLD-FINDERS

IN

ALTA CALIFORNIA:

BEING

THE DIARY OF AN EXPEDITION FROM SAN FRANCISCO
TO THE GOLD DISTRICTS.

BY

J. TYRWHITT BROOKS, M.D.

LONDON:
DAVID BOGUE, FLEET STREET.
MDCCCXLIX.

PREFACE.

THE accompanying diary—some interesting circumstances connected with which will be found in a letter
given at the end of the present volume—was sent
home by the Author merely for the entertainment of
the members of his own family and a few private
friends. It has been submitted to the public in
the hope that, as an authentic record of a variety
of interesting particulars connected with the original
discovery and present condition of the Gold Districts
of California, it will not fail to prove acceptable.

LONDON, 1849.

CONTENTS.

CHAPTER I.

CHAPTER II.

CHAPTER III.

CHAPTER IV.

CHAPTER V.

CHAPTER VI.

CHAPTER VII.

CHAPTER VIII.

CHAPTER XII.

CHAPTER XIII.

CHAPTER XIV.

CHAPTER XV.

CHAPTER XVI.

CHAPTER XVII.

CHAPTER XVIII.

CHAPTER XIX.

CHAPTER XX.

CHAPTER XXI.

CHAPTER XXII

CHAPTER XXIII.

CHAPTER XXIV.

CHAPTER XXV.

FOUR MONTHS

AMONG THE

GOLD-FINDERS IN ALTA CALIFORNIA,

CHAPTER I.

Clearing the Faranolles—Making the entrance to the Bay of San Francisco—
The passage through the Strait—Appearance of the Bay—Town of San
Francisco—The anchor is let go—The Author goes on shore—His bad
luck—Sweeting's Hotel—The Author and Mr. Malcolm propose visiting
the American settlements—They become acquainted with Captain Fulsom
and Mr. Bradley—Object of the Author's visit to California—Mr. M'Phail
leaves for Sonoma—The houses of San Francisco, and their inhabitants—
Native Californians—Senoritas and cigarettos.

* * * I felt heartily glad to hear that we were
then clearing the Faranolles, and soon hurried up on
deck, but we continued beating about for several hours
before we made the entrance to the Bay of San Francisco. At length, however, we worked our way in
between the two high bluffs, and along a strait a
couple of miles wide and nearly five miles long,

B

flanked on either side with bold broken hills—passing on our right hand the ricketty-looking fortifications erected by the Spaniards for the defence of the passage, but over which the Yankee stars and stripes were now floating. On leaving the strait we found ourselves on a broad sheet of rippling water looking like a great inland lake, hemmed in on all sides by lofty hills on which innumerable herds of cattle and horses were grazing, with green islands and clusters of rock rising up here and there, and a little fleet of ships riding at anchor. On our right was the town of San Francisco.

I had suffered so much from the voyage, that when the anchor was let go I felt no inclination to hurry on shore. M'Phail and Malcolm, however, went off, but promised to return to the ship that night. I soon after turned into my hammock, and, thanks to the stillness of the water in which we rode, slept soundly till morning.

April 29*th*.—This morning we all rose early, and went on shore. The little baggage we had we took in the boat. Malcolm told me that he had heard the war was over between the United States and Mexico, and I bitterly congratulated myself on ex-

periencing my usual run of bad luck. We made
our way to Sweeting's hotel, which Malcolm and
M'Phail had visited yesterday, and stated to be the
best of the three hotels which have sprung up here
since the Americans became masters of the place.

Malcolm intends making an excursion to the
interior. He proposes to visit the American settlements, and to satisfy himself as to the reputed
advantages which California presents as an agricul-
tural country. I have agreed to accompany him.
We have fallen in with two very pleasant American
gentlemen at our hotel to-day—one, a Captain Fulsom, holding some appointment under Government
here; the other, a young friend of his named Bradley.
We had some conversation together on the subject
of the Mexican war, in the course of which I learnt
that Mr. Bradley has been a resident in California
for the last eight years, and that he was one of the
officers of the volunteer corps attached to the army
of the United States, while military operations were
going on in this country. I told him of my desire
to enter as a surgeon in the service of the States,
and he promised to speak to Captain Fulsom on the
subject, and obtain from him a letter to Colonel

Mason, the new governor; but he is afraid there
is little chance of my meeting with success, as nearly
all the volunteer corps have been, or are about to be,
disbanded. Both Mr. Bradley and Captain Fulsom
speak very favourably of the climate and soil of
California, and say that an enterprising agriculturist
is sure to make a speedy fortune. Mr. Bradley, who
has agreed to accompany us on our trip, strongly
advises Malcolm to shift his quarters from Oregon,
and settle here, saying that he is sure my friend
will do so when he has once seen the farms in the
Sacramento valley, whither we are to start early next
week. M'Phail left us to-day, to make a trip to
Sonoma.

San Francisco, although as yet but a poor
place, will no doubt become a great emporium of
commerce. The population may be about a couple
of thousands; of these two-thirds are Americans.
The houses, with the exception of some few wooden
ones which have been shipped over here by the
Americans, are nearly all built of unburnt bricks.
The appearance of the native Californian is quite
Spanish. The men wear high steeple-like hats,
jackets of gaudy colours, and breeches of velvet,

generally cotton. They are a handsome, swarthy race. The best part in the faces of the women are their eyes, which are black and very lustrous. The Californian belles, I am sorry to say, spoil their teeth by smoking cigarettos.

CHAPTER II.

MONTEREY.

May 4th.—Started off early on the morning of the 2nd on our journey to Monterey. We found our horses in readiness in the hotel yard, in charge of a servant (here called a vaquero) of Mr. Bradley's. The latter, having business to transact at Monterey, accompanied us. My horse was equipped after the Spanish fashion, with the usual high-pommelled cumbrous saddle, with a great show of useless trappings, and clumsy wooden stirrups, and for a long time I found the riding sufficiently disagreeable, though, doubtless, far more pleasant than a coast journey would have been, with a repetition of the deadly sea-sickness from which I had already suffered so much. I soon found out, too, the advantages of the Spanish saddle, as enabling one to keep one's seat when travelling over the rough broken country through which our road ran. Bradley had told us to have our rifles in readiness, as no one travels any distance here without that very necessary protection, the mountains near the coast being infested with lawless gangs of ruffians, who lay in wait for solitary travellers.

The first part of our ride lay through a dense thicket of underwood, and afterwards across parched-up valleys, and over low sandy hills; then past large grazing grounds— where cattle might be counted by the thousand—and numerous ranchos or farms, the white farm buildings, surrounded by little garden patches, scattered over the hill sides. We at length came to an extensive plain, with groups of oaks spread over its surface, and soon afterwards reached the neglected Mission of Santa Clara, where we halted for a few hours. On leaving here our road was over a raised causeway some two or three miles in length, beneath an avenue of shady trees, which extended as far as the outskirts of the town of St. José. This town, or pueblo as it is called, is nothing more than a mass of ill-arranged and ill-built houses, with an ugly church and a broad plaza, peopled by three or four hundred inhabitants. Not being used to long journeys on horseback, I felt disposed to stop here for the night, but Bradley urged us to proceed a few miles farther, where we could take up our quarters at a rancho belonging to a friend of his. Accordingly we pushed on, and, after a ride of about seven miles, diverged from the main road, and soon reached the farm-house, where we were well entertained, and had a good night's rest.

Like the generality of houses in California, this was only one story high, and was built of piles driven into the ground, interlaced with boughs and sticks, and then plastered over with mud and whitewashed. The better class of farm-houses are built of adobes, or unburnt bricks, and tiled over.   The interior was as plain and cheerless as it well could be.   The floor was formed of the soil, beaten down till it was as firm and hard as a piece of stone.   The room set apart for our sleeping accommodation boasted as its sole ornaments a Dutch clock and a few gaudily-coloured prints of saints hung round the walls.   The beds were not over comfortable, but we were too

tired to be nice. In the morning I took a survey of
the exterior, and saw but few cattle stalled in the
sheds around the house. The greater part, it seems,
after being branded, are suffered to run loose over
the neighbouring pastures. There was a well-culti-
vated garden in the rear of the house, with abundance
of fruit trees and vegetables.

While we were at breakfast, Malcolm asked our
host several questions about his crops, and soon found
that he was no practical agriculturist. He had, however, at Bradley's suggestion, discarded the native
wooden plough for the more effective American
implement. He told us that he calculated his crop
of wheat this year would yield a hundred fanegas
for every one sown; and, on our expressing our
surprise at such a bountiful return, said that sixty or
over was the usual average. If so, the soil must be
something wonderful. After expressing our thanks,
for the hospitality shown us, to the wife of our host,
who was a very pretty little dark-eyed woman, with
a most winning way about her, we started off
to resume our journey. For my own part, I felt
very loth to proceed, for I was terribly fatigued by
my performance of yesterday, and suffered not a little

from that disagreeable malady called "saddle-sick-
ness." Our Californian accompanied us some short
distance on our road, which lay for many miles
through a wide valley, watered by a considerable
stream, and overgrown with oaks and sycamores.
Low hills rose on either hand, covered with dark
ridges of lofty pine trees, up which herds of elk and
deer were every now and then seen scampering. We
at length entered upon a narrow road through a range
of green sheltering hills, and, passing the Mission of
San Juan, crossed a wide plain and ascended the
mountain ridge which lay between us and Monterey,
where we arrived late in the day.

Next morning Mr. Bradley accompanied me to the
Governor's house, where we saw Colonel Mason, the
new governor of the State. He received us with
great politeness, but said that the war, if war it
deserved to be called, was now at an end, that but
a small number of troops were stationed in the
country, and that there was no vacancy for a surgeon.
" Indeed," he said, " considering that we have given up
head-breaking, and that the climate is proverbially
healthy, California is hardly the place for doctors to
settle in.—Besides," said he, " the Native Californians

all use the Temeschal (a sort of air bath) as a remedy
for every disorder." Colonel Mason than asked Mr.
Bradley if he had heard the reports of gold having
been found on the Sacramento, as Mr. Fulsom had
casually mentioned in a letter to him that such
rumours were prevalent at San Francisco. Bradley
replied that he had heard something about it, but
believed there was no truth in the matter, although
a few fools had indeed rushed off to the reputed
gold mines forthwith. With this our interview
terminated.

Monterey seems to be a rising town. The
American style of houses is superseding the old mud
structures, and numbers of new buildings are being
run up every month. The hotel we stopped at has
only been recently opened by an American. Monterey
is moreover a port of some importance, if one may
judge from the number of vessels lying at anchor.

May 7th.—On Friday we dined at the house of
Don Luis Palo, a Californian gentleman of agreeable
manners, whose father held office here under the
Spanish government previous to the Mexican Revolution. I believe it is Don Luis's intention shortly to
return to Spain. He is unmarried, and his two sisters

are the handsomest women I have yet seen in this country; their beauty is quite of the Spanish style. A dinner in California seems to be always the same— first soup and then beef, dressed in various ways, and seasoned with chillies; fowls, rice, and beans, with a full allowance of pepper and garlic to each dish.

On Saturday we set out on our return, and after two days' hard riding reached San Francisco to-day at 4, P. M.

CHAPTER III.

An arrival at San Francisco from the gold district—Captain Fulsom intends visiting the mine—The first Alcade and others examine the gold— Parties made up for the diggings—Newspaper reports—The Government officers propose taking possession of the mine—The Author and his friends decide to visit the Sacramento Valley—A horse is bought—Increase of the gold excitement—Work-people strike work and prepare to move off— Lawyers, store-keepers, and others follow their example—The Author's journey delayed— Ten dollars a day for a negro waiter—Waiting for a saddler—Don Luis Palo arrives from Monterey on his way to the mines— The report of the Government taking possession of the mines contradicted—Desertion of part of the Monterey garrison—Rumoured extent of the mines—The Author and his friends agree to go in company— Return of M'Phail—Preparations for the journey—" Gone to the diggings."

May 8th.—Captain Fulsom called at Sweeting's to-day. He had seen a man this morning who reported that he had just come from a river called the American Fork, about one hundred miles in the interior, where he had been gold washing. Captain Fulsom saw the gold he had with him ; it was about twenty-three ounces weight, and in small flakes. The man stated that he was eight days getting it, but Captain Fulsom hardly believed this. He says that he saw some of this gold a few weeks since, and thought it was only " mica," but good judges have pronounced it to be

genuine metal. He talks, however, of paying a visit to
the plaçe where it is reported to come from. After he
was gone Bradley stated that the Sacramento settlements, which Malcolm wished to visit, were in the
neighbourhood of the American Fork, and that we
might go there together : he thought the distance was
only one hundred and twenty miles.

May 10*th*.—Yesterday and to-day nothing has
been talked of but the new gold " placer," as people call
it. It seems that four other men had accompanied
the person Captain Fulsom saw yesterday, and that
they had each realized a large quantity of gold.
They left the " diggings" on the American Fork
(which it seems is the Rio de los Americanos, a tributary
to the Sacramento) about a week ago, and stopt a day
or two at Sutter's fort, a few miles this side of the
diggings, on their way : from there they had travelled
by boat to San Francisco. The gold they brought
has been examined by the first Alcalde here, and by
all the merchants in the place. Bradley showed us a
lump weighing a quarter of an ounce, which he had
bought of one of the men, and for which he gave him
three dollars and a half. I have no doubt in my own
mind about its being genuine gold. Several parties,

we hear, are already made up to visit the diggings; and, according to the newspaper here, a number of people have actually started off with shovels, mattocks, and pans to dig the gold themselves. It is not likely, however, that this will be allowed, for Captain Fulsom has already written to Colonel Mason about taking possession of the mine on behalf of the Government, it being, as he says, on public land.

May 13*th*.—It is now finally settled that we start off on Wednesday to the Sacramento Valley. To-day, under Bradley's direction, I have bought a good horse, for which I paid only fifteen dollars. It will be very little more expense than hiring a horse of the hotel-master here, besides being far more agreeable to have a horse of one's own; for everybody, the commonest workman even, rides in this country. The gold excitement increases daily, as several fresh arrivals from the mines have been reported at San Francisco. The merchants eagerly buy up the gold brought by the miners, and no doubt, in many cases, at prices considerably under its value. I have heard, though, of as much as sixteen dollars an ounce having been given in some instances, which I should have thought was over rather than under the full value of gold in

the United States. I confess I begin to feel seriously
affected with the prevailing excitement, and am
anxious for Wednesday to arrive.

May 17*th.*—This place is now in a perfect furor
of excitement; all the work-people have struck. Walking through the town to-day, I observed that labourers
were employed only upon about half-a-dozen of the
fifty new buildings which were in the course of being
run up.   The majority of the mechanics at this place
are making preparations for moving off to the mines,
and several hundred people of all classes—lawyers,
store-keepers, merchants, &c.—are bitten with the
fever; in fact, there is a regular gold mania
springing up.   I counted no less than eighteen
houses which were closed, the owners having left.
If Colonel Mason is moving a force to the American
Fork, as is reported here, their journey will be in
vain.

Our trip has been delayed to-day, for the saddler
cannot get our equipments in readiness for at least
forty-eight hours.   He says that directly he has
finished the job he shall start off himself to the
diggings. I have bribed him with promises of greatly
increased pay not to disappoint us again.   As it was,

we were to pay him a very high price, which he demanded on account of three of his men having left him, and there being only himself and two workmen to attend to our order.

I told Mr. Bradley of our misfortune. He promised to wait for us, but recommended me to keep going in and out of the saddlers all day long in order to make sure that the man was at work, otherwise we might be kept hanging about for a fortnight.

May 20th.—It requires a full amount of patience to stay quietly watching the proceedings of an inattentive tradesman amid such a whirlpool of excitement as is now in action. Sweeting tells me that his negro waiter has demanded and receives ten dollars a-day. He is forced to submit, for "helps" of all kinds are in great demand and very difficult to meet with. Several hundred people must have left here during the last few days. Malcolm and I have our baggage all in readiness to start on Monday.

May 22nd.—To-day all our arrangements have been changed ; the saddler did not keep his promise, and while Malcolm, Bradley, and myself were venting our indignation against him, Don Luis Palo made his appearance. The gold fever had spread to Monterey,

and he had determined to be off to the mines at once.
He had brought his servant (a converted Indian, named
José) with him, and extra horses with his baggage; he
intended to set to work himself at the diggings, and
meant to take everything he required with him.   He
says the report about Colonel Mason's moving a force
off to the mines to take possession of them is all
nonsense ; that some of the garrison of Monterey have
already gone there, is quite true, but they have
deserted to dig gold on their own account.   Colonel
Mason, he says, knows too well that he has no
efficient force for such a purpose, and that even if he
had, he would not be able to keep his men together.
It appears, also, that the mines occupy several miles of
ground, the gold not being confined to one particular
spot.   On hearing this intelligence we at once determined to follow Don Luis's example, and although
there seemed a certain degree of absurdity in four
people, all holding some position in society, going
off on what might turn out to be only a fool's errand,
still the evidence we had before us, of the gold which
had actually been found, and the example of the
multitudes who were daily hastening to the diggings,
determined us to go with the rest.   We therefore held

a council upon the best method of proceeding, at which every one offered his suggestions.

While we were thus engaged, M'Phail, our fellow-passenger from Oregon, made his appearance, having only just then returned from Sonoma. He had heard a great deal about the new gold placer, and he had merely come back for his baggage, intending to start off for the mines forthwith. The result of our deliberations was to this effect. Each man was to furnish himself with one good horse for his own use, and a second horse to carry his personal baggage as well as a portion of the general outfit; we were each to take a rifle, holster pistols, &c. It was agreed, moreover, that a tent should be bought immediately, if such a thing could be procured, as well as some spades, and mattocks, and a good stout axe, together with a collection of blankets and hides, and a supply of coffee, sugar, whisky, and brandy; knives, forks, and plates, with pots and kettles, and all the requisite cooking utensils for a camp life. The tent is the great difficulty, and fears are entertained that we shall not be able to procure one; but Bradley thinks he might buy one out of the Government stores.

I followed the saddler well up during the day,

and was fortunate enough to obtain our saddles, saddle-bags, &c. by four o'clock. On going to his house a couple of hours after about some trifling alteration I wished made, I found it shut up, and deserted. On the door was pasted a paper with the following words, " Gone to the diggings."

CHAPTER IV.

The party leave San Francisco—Cross to Sausalitto with horses and baggage —Appearance of the cavalcade—José's method of managing horses— Character of the country passed through—Stay at Sonoma for the night—A Yankee hotel-keeper's notion—The Author meets with Lieutenant Sherman —-Receives from him a letter of introduction to Captain Sutter—Napper Valley—Sleep at the house of a settler—Troublesome bedfellows—Wild-looking scenery—Bradley is injured by a fall from his horse—Difficulties in the way of pitching a tent—A hint to the bears—Supper and bed— Resume the journey—Sacramento valley—Elk and wild fowl—A long halt—A hunting party—A missing shot.

SONOMA.

May 24*th.*—This morning at last saw us off. We left San Francisco shortly after seven, and em- barked with our horses and baggage in a launch, which landed us at Sausalitto before ten. From thence we made our way to Sonoma, where we put up for the night. We formed quite a cavalcade, and presented a tolerably imposing appearance. First came the horses (six in number), which carried our baggage, camp equipments, &c. After these came José, Don Luis's Indian servant (who seems to be a far more lively fellow than Indians are generally), having these extra horses in his charge; and he really

managed them admirably. For what with whistling,
and coaxing, and swearing, and swinging his "riatta"
over their heads, he had them as much under his command, as ever a crack dragsman had his four-in-hand
in the good old coaching times of my own dear
England. We followed after, riding, when the road
would admit of it, all abreast, and presenting a bold
front to any gang of desperadoes who might be daring
enough to attack us. There was little fear of this, however, for we hardly rode a mile without falling in with
scattered parties bound to the gold mines.

We made our way but slowly during the first
portion of our ride, for the road wound up steep hills
and down into deep hollows, but when at last we came
upon a winding valley some miles in extent, our horses
got over the ground in a style which only Californian
steeds could achieve after the hard work which had
already been performed. Towards evening, we crossed
the hills which divided the valley from Sonoma plain,
and on reaching Sonoma put up at an hotel recently
opened here by a citizen from the United States, who
coolly told us, in the course of conversation, that he
guessed he didn't intend shearing off to the gold
mines, until he had drawn a few thousand dollars

from the San Francisco folk who pass through here
to and from the diggings.

May 27th.—We stopped at Sonoma the greater
part of Thursday, to give our horses rest.   At
the hotel, I met Lieutenant Sherman, who had
brought despatches to the officer in command here
from Colonel Mason.   I was much delighted in again
meeting with this gentleman, and we had a long talk
together over the merry times we had when we were
both staying at Washington.   When he heard our desti-
nation he kindly offered to give me a letter of introduction to a very old friend of his, Captain Sutter, the
proprietor of Sutter's fort, and one of the earliest
settlers on the Sacramento.   I availed myself of his
offer, and about three o'clock we started off across the
plain, and made our way through the groves of fine
oak trees which cover it in every direction.   We next
ascended the hills which lay between us and Napper
Valley, and after crossing them, made for the house of
an American settler, a friend of Bradley's, who pro-
vided us with the best accommodation his house would
furnish for the night.   We turned in early, but the
legions of fleas which were our bedfellows exerted
themselves to such a degree that for hours sleep was

out of the question.   The country is terribly plagued
with these vermin.   I do not know how the settlers
get on; perhaps they are accustomed to the infliction,
but a stranger feels it severely.

The next day we travelled over the corresponding
range of hills to those crossed on Thursday, and were
soon in the midst of a much wilder-looking country—
a rapid succession of steep and rugged mountains,
thickly timbered with tall pine trees and split up with
deep precipitous ravines, hemming in beautiful and
fertile valleys, brilliant with golden flowers and dotted
over with noble oaks.   While we were riding down
one of these dangerous chasms, Bradley, who was
showing off his superior equitation, was thrown from
his horse, and fell rather severely on his arm.   On
examining it, I was surprised to find he had escaped a
fracture.   As it is, he has injured it sufficiently to
prevent him from using the limb for several days.   I
bandaged it up, put it in a sling, and he proceeded in
a more cautious manner.

To-night we used our tent for the first time.   We
were somewhat awkward in pitching it, and three
times did the whole structure come down by the run,
burying several of us in the flapping canvas, and

inflicting some tolerably hard knocks with the poles. However, at length we succeeded in getting it fixed; and, kindling a blazing fire close to it, as a polite intimation to the bears that they were not wanted, cooked our supper over the embers, and then, wrapped in our blankets, slept far better than the fleas had allowed us to do the night before.

This morning I examined Bradley's arm, and was glad to find the inflammation somewhat reduced. He was bruised a good deal about the body generally, and complained to-day sorely of the pain he felt while being jolted over the broken ground which we crossed in our ascent of the tall mountains that bound the Sacramento Valley. From their summit we obtained a noble view of the broad winding river and its smaller tributaries, thickly studded with islands overgrown with noble oaks and sycamores. We encamped to-night at the foot of these hills, near a little stream which gurgled merrily by. We have seen several herds of elk to-day, and a large quantity of wild fowl.

Sunday, May 28th.—To-day we made a long halt, for we were all exceedingly tired, and some of our pack-horses, which were heavily laden, showed symptoms of " giving out." We determined, therefore, to stay here till late in the day, and then to follow the course of the creek for a few miles, and there pitch our tent. Turning our horses loose to graze, several of the party went off on a hunting excursion on foot, but their only success was about a score of wild geese, which are very plentiful in the marshy land bordering the creek. I got a shot at an elk which came down to the water to drink, but he made off unhurt.

CHAPTER V.

Encampment for the night—Symptoms of neighbours not far off—Reach the
Sacramento River—Sutter's Fort—Captain Sutter—His offer of accommodation—Various matters to be seen to—A walk through the Fort—Desertion
of the guard to the "diggings"—Work and whisky—Indians and their
bargains—A chief's effort to look like a civilized being—Yankee traders—
Indians and trappers—"Beats beaver skins"—Death to the weakest—A
regular Spanish Don and his servant—Captain Sutter a Swiss Guard—
His prejudice in favour of "constituted authorities."

May 29*th.*—Last night we encamped under a group
of oaks, and we "knew by the smoke that so
gracefully curled" over other parts of the valley, that
there were several other camps pitched at no great
distance. When we started in the morning we fell in
with a few parties moving towards the Sacramento.
A ride of a few hours brought us to the borders of
that noble river, which was here about a couple of
hundred yards wide, and we immediately made preparations for crossing it. After several mishaps and
delays, we at length succeeded in getting over in a
launch. The new town of Suttersville, numbering
some ten or twelve houses, is laid out within half a
mile of the banks of the river. From here a brisk

ride over a level plain—parcelled out into fields of
wheat and pasture-grounds, dotted with hundreds upon
hundreds of grazing cattle, and here and there a loiter-
ing team—brought us to Sutter's Fort, an extensive
block of building planted on the top of a small hill
which skirts a creek running into the Americanos,
near its junction with the Rio Sacramento. A
schooner and some small craft were beating up the
Americanos River towards the Fort, and alongside
the landing-place several launches were lying un-
shipping cargoes. As we made the spot, we soon
saw that here all was bustle and activity. Boat-
men were shouting and swearing; wagoners were
whistling and hallooing and cracking their whips at
their straining horses, as these toiled along with
heavily-laden wagons to the different stores within the
building; groups of horsemen were riding to and
fro, and crowds of people were moving about on foot.
It was evident that the gold mania increased in force
as we approached the now eagerly longed for El
Dorado.

On inquiring of a squaw we met at the entrance of
the Fort, and who knew just sufficient English to
understand our question, she pointed out to us as

Captain Sutter a very tall good-looking sort of per-
sonage, wearing a straw hat and loose coat and trowsers
of striped duck, but with features as unlike those of
a Yankee as can well be imagined. I at once introduced myself, and handed him the letter which
Lieutenant Sherman had given me. After reading it,
the Captain informed me that he was happy enough to
see me, although he feared, from the great change
which a few weeks had made in this part of the world,
that he could offer me but indifferent hospitality.
Every store and shed was being crammed with bales
of goods, barrels of flour, and a thousand other things
for which a demand has suddenly spung up. The
Captain's own house was indeed just like an hotel
crowded with many more visitors than it could accommodate; still no one who came there, so the Captain
was good enough to say, recommended by his friend
Sherman, should have other than an hospitable recep-
tion. All that he could do, however, he said, would be
to place one sleeping-room at my service for myself and
such of my friends as I liked to share it with; and,
leaving me to arrange the matter with them, he went
away, promising to return and show us our quarters.

I told my companions of the Captain's offer, but

they were satisfied to rough it out of doors again to-
night, and it was arranged that only Bradley and
myself should accept the sleeping accommodation
offered by Captain Sutter, as a good night's rest in
comfortable quarters would be more beneficial to our
friend with the injured limb, than an out-door nap
with a single blanket for a bed and a saddle for a
pillow.

Two of our horses having cast their shoes, Malcolm
and José walked them round to the blacksmith's shop,
where, after their losses were repaired, a stock of shoes,
nails, &c. were to be laid in for future contingencies.
M'Phail and our Spanish friend undertook at the same
time to purchase a ten days' supply of provisions for
us, and Bradley agreed to look about the Fort and
see if he could meet with another servant. In this
errand, I am sorry to say, he was not successful.

While these several commissions were executing,
the Captain returned and walked with me through the
Fort. On our way he pointed out the guard-house,
the Indian soldiers attached to which had deserted to
the mines almost to a man; the woollen factory, with
some thirty women still at work; the distillery
house, where the famous pisco is made; and the black-

smiths' and wheelwrights' shops, with more work before them than the few mechanics left will be able to get through in a month. Yet all these men talked of starting off to the diggings in a day or two. The Captain told me he had only been able to keep them by greatly increased pay, and by an almost unlimited allowance of pisco and whisky.

It was not easy to pick our way through the crowds of strange people who were moving backwards and forwards in every direction. Carts were passing to and fro; groups of Indians squatting on their haunches were chattering together, and displaying to one another the flaring red and yellow handkerchiefs, the scarlet blankets, and muskets of the most worthless Brummagem make, for which they had been exchanging their bits of gold, while their squaws looked on with the most perfect indifference. I saw one chief, who had gone for thirty years with no other covering than a rag to hide his nakedness, endeavouring to thrust his legs into a pair of sailor's canvas trowsers with very indifferent success.

Inside the stores the bustle and noise were even greater. Some half-a-dozen sharp-visaged Yankees, in straw hats and loose frocks, were driving hard bargains for dollars with the crowds of customers who were continually pouring in to barter a portion of their stock of gold for coffee and tobacco, breadstuff, brandy, and bowie knives ; of spades and mattocks there were none to be had. In one corner, at a railed-off desk, a quick-eyed old man was busily engaged, with weights and scales, setting his own value on the lumps of golden ore or the bags of dust which were being handed over to him, and in exchange for which he told out the estimated quantity of dollars. These dollars quickly returned to the original deposit, in payment for goods bought at the other end of the store.

Among the clouds of smoke puffed forth by some score of pipes and as many cigarettos, there were to be seen, mingled together, Indians of various degrees of civilization, and corresponding styles of dress, varying from the solitary cloth kilt to the cotton shirts and jackets and trowsers of Russia duck; with groups of trappers from as far up as Oregon, clad in coats of buffalo hide, and with faces and hands so brown and wrinkled that one would take their skins to be as tough as the buffalo's, and almost as indifferent to a lump of lead. " Captain," said one of these gentry, shaking a bag of gold as we passed, " I guess this beats beaver skins—eh, captain?" Another of them, who had a savage-looking wolf-dog with him, was holding a palaver with an Indian from the borders of the Klamath Lake; and the most friendly understanding seemed to exist between them. " You see those two scoundrels?" said the Captain to me. " They look and talk for all the world like brothers, but only let either of them get the chance of a shot at the other after scenting his trail, may be for days, across those broad hunting-grounds, where every man they meet they look upon as a foe, and the one that has the quickest eye and the readiest hand will alone live to see the sun rise next day."

Threading his way amongst the crowd, I was somewhat struck by the appearance of a Spanish Don of the old school, looking as magnificent as a very gaudy light blue jacket with silver buttons and scarlet trimmings, and breeches of crimson velvet, and striped silk sash, and embroidered deer-skin shoes, and a perfumed cigaretto could make him. He wore his slouched sombrero jauntily placed on one side, and beneath it, of course, the everlasting black silk handkerchief, with the corners dangling over his neck behind.

Following him was his srevant, in slouched hat and
spangled garters, carrying an old Spanish musket over
his shoulder, and casting somewhat timid looks at the
motley assemblage of Indians and trappers, who every
now and then jostled against him.   Beyond these,
there were a score or two of go-a-head Yankees—
"gentlemen traders," I suppose they called themselves—
with a few pretty Californian women, who are on their
way with their husbands to the mines.   I noticed that
the Captain had a word for almost every one, and that
he seemed to be held in very great respect.

Bradley informed me to-night of the origin of a
scar which is just distinguishable in Captain Sutter's
face.   It seems that the Captain, who is a Swiss, was
one of Charles the Tenth's guards in 1830, and that a
slight cut from the sabre of one of the youths of the
Polytechnic School had left in his visage a standing
memorial of the three glorious days.   Indeed the
Captain seems generally to have taken the side of the
constituted authorities, as in the revolution of 1845 he
turned out with all his people for the Mexican Government.   However, he was more fortunate in California
than in Paris, as he did n't even get his skin scratched
on this occasion.

CHAPTER VI.

The journey delayed—A walk to the camp—A list of wants—Captain Sutter's account of his first settlement in California—How he served the Indians, and how he civilized them—Breakfast—Captain Sutter's wife and daughter —Ridiculous stories about the discovery of the gold mines—Joe Smith's prophecy—An Indian ghost—Something about a ship-load of rifles.

May 30*th*.—To my great disappointment, our journey was not resumed to-day. As I had expected, Malcolm had found there was no chance of getting the farrier's assistance yesterday, and he came to me in the evening to inform me that he and the rest were going into camp for the night. Bradley and myself found an ample supper prepared for us; and after doing due justice to the eatables, and dressing Bradley's arm, I shortened the night a couple of hours by jotting down the events of the day.

This morning I rose early, and walked to the camp, which I found, about half a mile off, under some oaks in a piece of pasture land on the Captain's farm. I had some difficulty in finding it out, for there were at least fifteen or twenty tents of one kind or another in the "bottom." The party were all roused, and breakfast

was preparing under Don Luis's superintendence. It
was the general opinion that we must buy two extra
horses to carry our breadstuffs, &c. Malcolm reported
that there were a variety of articles we were still in
want of; namely, tin drinking cups, some buckets for
water, with forks, and other small articles. He recommended that a couple more axes and a strong saw be
bought at Brannan's, together with hammers, nails, &c.,
and some of the Indian baskets which seem to be so
common about here.

On my return to the Fort, I fell in with the
Captain, rigged out in a military undress uniform. I
chatted with him for half an hour about his farm, &c.
He told me he was the first white man who settled in
this part of the country ; that some ten years ago,
when the Mexican Government was full of colonization
schemes, the object of which was to break up the
Missions, and to introduce a population antagonistic
to the Californians, he received a grant of land, sixty
miles one way and twelve another, about sixteen or
seventeen hundred acres of which he had now brought
under cultivation. " When I came here," said the Captain, " I knew the country and the Indians well. Eight
years ago these fields were overgrown with long rank

grass, with here and there an oak or pine sprouting
out from the midst. You can see what they are now.
As to the Indians, they gave me a little more trouble.
I can boast of fourteen pieces of cannon, though one
has little occasion for them now, except to fire a few
salutes on days of rejoicing. Well! most of these
guns came from Ross within this last four years ; but
when I first arrived here, I brought with me a couple
of howitzers, from which one night, when these
thieves were hemming me in on all sides, I discharged
a shell right over their heads. The mere sight of it,
when it bursted, was sufficient to give them a very
respectful notion of the fighting means at my command. But though this saved me from any direct
attack, it did not secure me against having my horses
and cattle stolen on every convenient occasion." The
Captain went on to say, that he at last brought the
Indians pretty well under control ; and that, by
promises of articles of clothing, they became willing
to work for him. He took good care to trust very
few of them with rifles or powder and shot. Nearly
every brick in the buildings of the Fort, he tells me,
was made by the Indians, who, moreover, dug all the
ditches dividing his wheat fields. These ditches are

very necessary, to prevent the large number of cattle and horses on the farm from straying among the crops.

On our way to the house, I got the Captain to speak to the head blacksmith about our horses, after which we went into breakfast, when I saw his wife and daughter for the first time. They are both very lady-like women, and both natives of France. During the meal, I found Captain Sutter communicative on the subject of the discovery of the gold mines, which I was glad of, as I was anxious to learn the true particulars of the affair, respecting which so many ridiculous stories had been circulated. One was to the effect, that the mines had been discovered by the Mormons, in accordance with a prophecy made by the famous Joe Smith. Another tale was, that the Captain had seen the apparition of an Indian chief, to whom he had given a rifle (the possession of which he only lived three months to enjoy, having been trampled down by a buffalo in the neighbourhood of the Rocky Mountains, on his way with his tribe to make an attack on the Pawnees), when the ghost in question told the Captain that he would make him very rich, and begged that, with this promised cash, the Captain would immediately buy a ship-load of rifles, and present one to

every member of his tribe.   Such were the absurd
stories circulated.   The true account of the discovery
I here give, as near as I can recollect, in the Captain's
own words.

CHAPTER VII.

"I WAS sitting one afternoon," said the Captain,
" just after my siesta, engaged, by-the-bye, in writing
a letter to a relation of mine at Lucerne, when I was
interrupted by Mr. Marshall—a gentleman with whom
I had frequent business transactions—bursting hurriedly
into the room. From the unusual agitation in his
manner I imagined that something serious had occurred, and, as we involuntarily do in this part of the
world, I at once glanced to see if my rifle was in its
proper place. You should know that the mere appearance of Mr. Marshall at that moment in the Fort was

quite enough to surprise me, as he had but two days
before left the place to make some alterations in a mill
for sawing pine planks, which he had just run up for
me, some miles higher up the Americanos. When he
had recovered himself a little, he told me that, however
great my surprise might be at his unexpected reappear-
ance, it would be much greater when I heard the
intelligence he had come to bring me. 'Intelligence,'
he added, 'which, if properly profited by, would put
both of us in possession of unheard-of wealth—millions
and millions of dollars, in fact.' I frankly own, when
I heard this, that I thought something had touched
Marshall's brain, when suddenly all my misgivings
were put an end to by his flinging on the table a
handful of scales of pure virgin gold. I was fairly
thunderstruck, and asked him to explain what all this
meant, when he went on to say, that, according to my
instructions, he had thrown the mill-wheel out of gear,
to let the whole body of the water in the dam find a
passage through the tail-race, which was previously too
narrow to allow the water to run off in sufficient
quantity, whereby the wheel was prevented from effi-
ciently performing its work. By this alteration the
narrow channel was considerably enlarged, and a mass

of sand and gravel carried off by the force of the
torrent.   Early in the morning after this took place,
he (Mr. Marshall) was walking along the left bank of
the stream, when he perceived something which he at
first took for a piece of opal—a clear transparent stone,
very common here—glittering on one of the spots laid
bare by the sudden crumbling away of the bank.   He
paid no attention to this; but while he was giving
directions to the workmen, having observed several
similar glittering fragments, his curiosity was so far
excited, that he stooped down and picked one of them
up.   'Do you know,' said Mr. Marshall to me, 'I
positively debated within myself two or three times
whether I should take the trouble to bend my back to
pick up one of the pieces, and had decided on not
doing so, when, further on, another glittering morsel
caught my eye—the largest of the pieces now before
you.   I condescended to pick it up, and to my astonishment found that it was a thin scale of what appears
to be pure gold.'   He then gathered some twenty or
thirty similar pieces, which on examination convinced
him that his suppositions were right.   His first impres-
sion was, that this gold had been lost or buried there
by some early Indian tribe—perhaps some of those

mysterious inhabitants of the west, of whom we have
no account, but who dwelt on this continent centuries
ago, and built those cities and temples, the ruins of
which are scattered about these solitary wilds.   On
proceeding, however, to examine the neighbouring
soil, he discovered that it was more or less auriferous.
This at once decided him.   He mounted his horse,
and rode down to me as fast as it would carry him
with the news.

"At the conclusion of Mr. Marshall's account,"
continued Captain Sutter, "and when I had convinced
myself, from the specimens he had brought with him,
that it was not exaggerated, I felt as much excited as
himself.   I eagerly inquired if he had shown the gold
to the work-people at the mill, and was glad to hear
that he had not spoken to a single person about it.
We agreed," said the Captain, smiling, "not to mention the circumstance to any one, and arranged to set
off early the next day for the mill.   On our arrival,
just before sundown, we poked the sand about in
various places, and before long succeeded in collecting
between us more than an ounce of gold, mixed up with
a good deal of sand.   I stayed at Mr. Marshall's that
night, and the next day we proceeded some little dis-

tance up the South Fork, and found that gold existed along the whole course, not only in the bed of the main stream, where the water had subsided, but in every little dried-up creek and ravine.   Indeed I think it is more plentiful in these latter places, for I myself, with nothing more than a small knife, picked out from a dry gorge, a little way up the mountain, a solid lump of gold which weighed nearly an ounce and a half.

" On our return to the mill, we were astonished by the work-people coming up to us in a body, and showing us small flakes of gold similar to those we had ourselves procured. Marshall tried to laugh the matter off with them, and to persuade them that what they had found was only some shining mineral of trifling value; but one of the Indians, who had worked at the gold mine in the neighbourhood of La Paz, in Lower California, cried out, 'Oro! oro!' We were disappointed enough at this discovery, and supposed that the work-people had been watching our movements, although we thought we had taken every precaution against being observed by them. I heard afterwards, that one of them, a sly Kentuckian, had dogged us about, and that, looking on the ground to see if he could discover

what we were in search of, he had lighted on some
flakes of gold himself.

" The next day I rode back to the Fort, organised
a labouring party, set the carpenters to work on a few
necessary matters, and the next day accompanied them
to a point of the Fork, where they encamped for the
night. By the following morning I had a party of
fifty Indians fairly at work. The way we first
managed was to shovel the soil into small buckets, or
into some of our famous Indian baskets; then wash all
the light earth out, and pick away the stones ; after this,
we dried the sand on pieces of canvas, and with long
reeds blew away all but the gold. I have now some
rude machines in use, and upwards of one hundred
men employed, chiefly Indians, who are well fed, and
who are allowed whisky three times a-day.

"The report soon spread. Some of the gold was sent
to San Francisco, and crowds of people flocked to the
diggings. Added to this, a large emigrant party of
Mormons entered California across the Rocky Mountains, just as the affair was first made known. They
halted at once, and set to work on a spot some thirty
miles from here, where a few of them still remain.
When I was last up at the diggings, there were full

eight hundred men at work, at one place and another, with perhaps something like three hundred more passing backwards and forwards between here and the mines. I at first imagined the gold would soon be exhausted by such crowds of seekers, but subsequent observations have convinced me that it will take many years to bring about such a result, even with ten times the present number of people employed.

" What surprises me," continued the Captain, " is, that this country should have been visited by so many scientific men, and that not one of them should have ever stumbled upon these treasures; that scores of keen-eyed trappers should have crossed this valley in every direction, and tribes of Indians have dwelt in it for centuries, and yet that this gold should have never been discovered. I myself have passed the very spot above a hundred times during the last ten years, but was just as blind as the rest of them, so I must not wonder at the discovery not having been made earlier."

While the Captain was proceeding with his narrative, I must confess that I felt so excited on the subject as to wish to start off immediately on our journey. When he had finished, I walked off to see after the horses, but, although they were ready, the additional shoes we wanted to carry with us, would not be furnished for several hours : it was late in the afternoon before we got them. We bought two horses of Captain Sutter (very strong animals), and M'Phail managed to engage a big lad as a servant—a rough-looking fellow, who appears to have deserted from some ship, and worked his way up here. All things considered, it was agreed that we should remain here another night, and resume our march as early as we could in the morning.

CHAPTER VIII.

The Author and his friends leave Sutter's Fort — Tents in the bottom—A
caravan in motion—Green hills and valleys — Indian villages — Californian pack - horses — A sailor on horseback — Lunch at noon —A
troublesome beast—Sierra Nevada — First view of the lower mines—
How the gold is dug and washed—The " cradle "—The diggers and their
stock of gold — A store in course of construction—The tent is pitched—
The golden itch—First attempts at gold-finding—A hole in the saucepan
—Sound asleep.

Sunday, June 4th.—The morning we left the Fort
the scene was one of great excitement.   Down in the
bottom some twenty tents were pitched, outside which
big fires were smoking ; and, while breakfast was
being prepared, the men of each company were busily
engaged in saddling their horses and arranging their
baggage ; several wagons and teams were already in
motion, following the road along the windings of the
river.   The tents were soon all struck, the smoke
from the fires was dying away, and a perfect caravan
was moving along in the direction of the now no
longer ridiculed El Dorado.

We pushed along, as may be believed, with the
utmost impatience, conjuring up the most flattering

visions of our probable success as gold-hunters. The track lay through a spacious grassy valley, with the Americanos River winding along it, on our left hand. At first, the stream was nearly two miles distant from the track of our caravan, but as we advanced we approached its banks more nearly. The country was pleasant, consisting of a succession of small hills and valleys, diversified here and there by groves of tall oak trees. We passed several wretched Indian villages—clusters of filthy smoky hovels, and now and then caught sight of the river and the line of oak trees which bordered it. We managed tolerably well with our horses, but it requires great experience to be able to fasten securely the loads of provisions and stores which they carry on their backs. Flour, of course, formed the principal article of our commissariat. This was packed up in sacks, which were again enclosed in long pockets, made of hides, and called " parfleshes," the use of which is to defend the canvas of the sacking from being torn by branches of fern and underwood. The sacks we secured on strong pack-saddles, between which and the back of the horse were some thick soft cloths. All our baggage-horses were furnished with trail ropes, which were allowed to drag on the ground after the horse, for the purpose of enabling us to catch him more readily. Besides the animals we rode, we had seven horses, for the conveyance of our provisions, tents, &c. The two we bought from Captain Sutter, though strong, were skittish, and gave us much trouble, for our newly engaged servant, whose name is James Horry, knew more about harpooning and flenching whales than about the management of horses. He was certainly willing and did his best, but he occasioned some mirth during the day's march by his extreme awkwardness on horseback. However, to do him justice, he bore the numerous falls which he came in for with great philosophy, starting up again every time he was " grassed," and laughing as loudly as the rest.

At noon we halted to refresh by the side of a small stream of crystal purity. While making preparations for our hurried meal, we had all our eyes about us for gold in the channel of the rivulet, but saw none. We had not yet reached the favoured spot. After some difficulty in catching the pack-horses, one of the perverse brutes having taken it into its head to march up to its belly in the stream, where he floundered about for some time, enjoying the coolness of the water, we

set forward, determined to reach the lower diggings
by sundown.   As we neared the spot the ground
gradually became more broken and heavily timbered
with oak and pine, while in the distance, and separated from us by deep forests of these trees, might be
seen a long ridge of snow-capped mountains — the
lofty Sierra Nevada.   But we were too anxious to
reach the gold to care much about the more unpro-
fitable beauties of Nature, and accordingly urged our
horses to the quickest speed they could put forth.
We were now travelling along the river's banks, and
towards evening came in sight of the lower mines,
here called the " Mormon " diggings, which occupy
a surface of two or three miles along the river.   There
were something like forty tents scattered up the hill
sides, occupied mostly by Americans, some of whom
had brought their families with them.   Although it
was near sundown, everybody was in full occupation.
At every few yards there were men, with their naked
arms, busily employed in washing out the golden
flakes and dust from spadefuls of the auriferous soil.
Others were first passing it through sieves, many of
them freshly made with intertwisted willow branches,
to get rid of the coarse stones, and then washing the

lumps of soil in pots placed beneath the surface of
the water, the contents of the vessel being kept continually stirred by the hand until the lighter particles
of earth or gravel were carried away.

A great number of the settlers, however, were
engaged in making what are here called " cradles;"
partly, I suppose, from their shape, and partly from
the rocking motion to which they are subjected.
These machines were being roughly constructed of
deal boards.   Later in the day I watched one of them
at work, and had the process explained to me.   Four
men were employed at it.   The first shovelled up the
earth; another carried it to the cradle, and dashed it
down on a grating or sieve—placed horizontally at
the head of the machine—the wires of which, being
close together, only allowed the smaller particles of
earth and sand to fall through ; the third man
rocked the cradle—I must confess I never saw one so
perseveringly rocked at home ; while the fourth kept
flinging water upon the mass of earth inside.   The
result of this four-fold process is, that the lighter
earth is gradually carried off by the action of the
water, and a sort of thick black sediment of sand is
left at the bottom of the cradle.   This was afterwards

scooped out, and put aside to be carefully dried in the sun to-morrow morning.

I can hardly describe the effect this sight produced upon our party. It seemed as if the fabled treasure of the Arabian Nights had been suddenly realised before us. We all shook hands, and swore to preserve good faith with each other, and to work hard for the common good. The gold-finders told us that some of them frequently got as much as fifty dollars a-day. As we rode from camp to camp, and saw the hoards of gold—some of it in flakes, but the greater part in a coarse sort of dust—which these people had amassed during the last few weeks, we felt in a perfect fluster of excitement at the sight of the wealth around us. One man showed us four hundred ounces of pure gold dust which he had washed from the dirt in a tin pan, and which he valued at fourteen dollars an ounce.

As may be imagined, the whole scene was one well calculated to take a strong hold upon the imagination. The eminences, rising gradually from the river's banks, were dotted with white canvas tents, mingled with the more sombre-looking huts, constructed with once green but now withered branches. A few hundred yards from the river lay a large heap

of planks and framings, which I was told were intended for constructing a store; the owner of which,
a sallow Yankee, with a large pluffy cigaretto in his
mouth, was labouring away in his shirt sleeves.

Bewildered and excited by the novelty of the
scene, we were in haste to pitch our camp, and soon
fixed upon a location. This was by the side of a
dried-up water-course, through which, in the wet
season, a small rivulet joined the larger stream; we
did not, however, immediately set to work to make
the necessary arrangements for the night. Our fingers
were positively itching for the gold, and in less
than half an hour after our arrival, the pack-horse
which carried the shovels, scoops, and pans, had been
released of his burden, and all our party were as busily
employed as the rest. As for myself, armed with a
large scoop or trowel, and a shallow tin pail, I leapt
into the bed of the rivulet, at a spot where I perceived
no trace of the gravel and earth having been artificially
disturbed. Near me was a small clear pool, which
served for washing the gold. Some of our party
set to work within a short distance of me, while others
tried their fortune along the banks of the Americanos,
digging up the shingle which lay at the very brink

of the stream. I shall not soon forget the feeling with which I first plunged my scoop into the soil beneath me. Half filling my tin pail with the earth and shingle, I carried it to the pool, and placing it beneath the surface of the water, I began to stir it with my hand, as I had observed the other diggers do. Of course I was not very expert at first, and I dare say I flung out a good deal of the valuable metal. However, I soon perceived that the earth was crumbling away, and was being carried by the agitation of the water into the pool, which speedily became turbid, while the sandy sediment of which I had heard remained at the bottom of the pail. Carefully draining the water away, I deposited the sand in one of the small close-woven Indian baskets we had brought with us, with the intention of drying it at the camp fire, there not being sufficient time before nightfall to allow the moisture gradually to absorb by the evaporation of the atmosphere.

After working for about half an hour, I retraced my steps with my basket to the spot where we had tethered the horses, and found the animals still standing there with their burdens on their backs. Mr. Malcolm was already there; he had with him about an equal quantity of the precious black sand ; it remained, however, to be seen what proportion of gold our heaps contained. In a short time Bradley and Don Luis joined us, both of them in tip-top spirits. " I guess this is the way we do the trick down in these clearings," said the former, shaking a bag of golden sand. As for José, Don Luis's Indian servant, he was devout in his expressions of thanksgiving to the Virgin Mary and the Great Spirit, whom he would insist upon classifying together, in a most remarkable and not quite orthodox manner.

We now set to work to get up our tent. Malcolm, in the meantime, prepared coffee and very under-baked cakes, made of the flour we had brought with us. His cooking operations were greatly impeded by our eagerness to dry the sand we had scraped up —a feat in the achievement of which Bradley was clumsy enough to burn a hole in our very best sauce-pan. However, we managed to get the moisture absorbed, and, shutting our eyes, we commenced blowing away the sand with our mouths, and shortly after found ourselves the possessors of a few pinches of gold. This was encouraging for a beginning. We drank our coffee in high spirits, and then, having picketted our horses, made ourselves as snug as our accommodation would allow, and, being tired out, not only with the journey and the work, but with excitement and anxiety, slept soundly till morning.

CHAPTER IX.

Two horses stray away—How orders were enforced at the diggings—Sunday
work—Nature of the soil—Inconveniences even in gold getting—Dinner
and rest—A strike for higher wages—A walk through the diggings—Sleeping and smoking—Indians and finery—Californians and Yankees—Run-
away sailors and stray negroes—A native-born Kentuckian—"That's a
fact"—A chapel at the diggings—A supper with an appetite.

THE morning broke brilliantly, and the first thing
we discovered on rising was, that two of the horses
had broken their fastenings during the night, and
strayed. As we could not afford to lose the animals,
José and Horry were despatched to look after them,
and they grumbled not a little at being thus sent off
from the scene of golden operations; but Bradley,
producing a rifle, swore that he would shoot them
both unless they obeyed orders; so, after a little
altercation, away they went.

Breakfast was soon despatched, and the question
as to the day's operations asked. Don Luis was the
only one who, on the score of its being Sunday,
would not go to the diggings. He had no objection
to amuse himself on Sunday, but he would not work.

To get over the difficulty, we agreed to go upon the principle of every man keeping his own findings, our bonds of unity as a party to extend merely to mutual protection and defence. Leaving Don Luis, then, smoking in the tent, we proceeded to work, and found that the great majority of the gold-finders appeared to entertain our opinions, or at all events to imitate our practice, as to labouring on the Sunday. I had now leisure more particularly to remark the nature of the soil in which the gold was found. The dust is found amid the shingle actually below water, but the most convenient way of proceeding is to take the soil from that portion of the bed which has been overflowed but is now dry. It is principally of a gravelly nature, full of small stones, composed, as far as I could make out, of a species of jasper and milky quality, mingled with fragments of slate and splinters of basalt. The general opinion is, that the gold has been washed down from the hills.

I worked hard, as indeed we all did, the whole morning. The toil is very severe, the constant stooping pressing, of course, upon the spinal column, whilst the constant immersion of the hands in water causes the skin to excoriate and become exceedingly painful. But these inconveniences are slight when compared to the great gain by which one is recompensed for them.

At twelve o'clock, our usual primitive dinner hour, we met at the tents, tolerably well tired with our exertions. No dinner, however, was prepared, both José and Horry being still absent in pursuit of the strayed horses. We had, therefore, to resort to some of our jerked beef, which, with biscuits and coffee, formed our fare. After dinner, we determined to rest until the next day. The fact is, that the human frame will not stand, and was never intended to stand, a course of incessant toil; indeed, I believe that in civilized—that is to say, in industrious—communities, the Sabbath, bringing round as it does a stated remission from labour, is an institution physically necessary.

We therefore passed some time in conversation, which was interrupted by the arrival of José and Horry with the strayed horses. Horry demanded an immediate increase of wages, threatening to leave us and set to work on his own account if we refused. Bradley tried to talk big and bully him, but in vain.

José had a sort of fear of Don Luis—who in return looked on his servant as his slave—so he said nothing. We could see, however, that they had evidently been in communication with the diggers around, and so we gave in. Later in the afternoon I started with Malcolm and M'Phail for a walk through the diggings. We found comparatively a small proportion of the people who had commenced work in the morning still at their pans. Numbers were lying asleep under the trees, or in the shade of their tents and wagons. Others sat smoking and chatting in circles upon the grass, mending their clothes or performing other little domestic duties at the same time. It was really a motley scene. Indians strutted by in all the pride of gaudy calico, the manners of the savage concealed beneath the dress of the civilized man. Muscular sun-burnt fellows, whose fine forms and swarthy faces pronounced that Spanish blood ran through their veins, gossiped away with sallow, hatchet-faced Yankees, smart men at a bargain, and always on the look-out for squalls. Here and there one spied out the flannel shirt and coarse canvas trowsers of a seaman—a run-away, in all probability, from a South Sea whaler; while one or two stray negroes chattered with all the

volubility of their race, shaking their woolly heads
and showing their white teeth. I got into conversation
with one tall American; he was a native-born Kentuckian, and full of the bantam sort of consequence of his
race. He predicted wonderful things from the discovery of the mineral treasures of California, observing
that it would make a monetary revolution all over the
world, and that nothing similar, at least to so great an
extent, was ever known in history. "Look around! for,
stranger," said he to me, " I guess you don't realise
such a scene every day, and that's a fact. There's gold
to be had for the picking of it up, and by all who
choose to come and work. I reckon old John Bull
will scrunch up his fingers in his empty pockets when
he comes to hear of it. It's a most everlasting wonderful thing, and that's a fact, that beats Joe Dunkin's
goose-pie and apple sarse."

Farther on we came upon a tremendous-looking
tent, formed by two or three tents being flung into
one, which, on examination, we found was doing
duty as a chapel. A missionary, from one of the
New England States, as I hear, was holding forth
to a pretty large congregation. The place was very
hot and chokey, and I only stayed long enough to

hear that the discourse abounded in the cloudy metaphors and vague technicalities of Calvinistic theology.

The remainder of the afternoon I have been devoting to writing my journal, which I here break off to commence a hearty good supper, in revenge for the scrambling sort of dinner one has had to-day. The beef does n't look roasted as they would put it on the table at the Clarendon, or at Astor House even ; but none of those who sit down to the Clarendon table, at any rate, have such an appetite as I now have, far away beyond care and civilization, in the gold-gathering region of California.

CHAPTER X.

Digging and washing, with a few reflections—A cradle in contemplation—
Scales to sell, but none to lend—Stock of gold weighed—More arrivals—
Two new-comers—Mr. Biggs and Mr. Lacosse—Good order prevails at
the mines—Timber bought for the cradles—The cradles made—The cradles
worked—The result of the first day's trial.

June 5th.—We have laboured hard all day, digging and washing, and with good success. I begin to hope now that I have really laid the foundation of a fortune, and I thank God for it. I have
been kicked tolerably well about the world, and the
proverb, that a " rolling stone gathers no moss," has,
I am sure, been abundantly proved by my case.
Now, however, I have a grand chance, and I am
resolved that all that industry and perseverance can
do shall be done to improve it.

Before starting for work this morning, it was
agreed that José should act as cook for the day; it
being stipulated that he was to have the afternoon
to himself for digging. Horry was left in charge
of the horses. I worked hard, keeping near Bradley,
and conversing with him as I shovelled the gravel

into the pail, and stirred it about in the clear pools.
We had very fair success, but still we could not but
think that this was a poor way of proceeding; besides, I didn't like the back-breaking work of stooping all day. I therefore proposed that we should
endeavour to knock up a cradle. The expense for
wood would certainly be great, but it would be better
to incur it than keep to the present rude and toilsome
plan of operation.

We proposed the plan to our comrades at dinner-
time, and it was, on the whole, well received.
Malcolm and M'Phail entered into the notion, and
we determined to try whether we could not put forth
sufficient carpentering ability to carry it out. The
next day was fixed upon for commencing the work.

After dinner we returned to our shovels and pails.
In the evening we were anxious to know how much
gold we had realised by our labours up to the present
time; and, accordingly, I set off to borrow a pair
of scales. After entering several tents in vain, I was
directed to the Yankee who had the materials for a
store, and whose name was Hiram Ensloe. He had
several pairs to sell, but none to lend. I asked his
prices, and now had, for the first time, a real example

of the effects of plenty of gold and scarcity of goods.
For a small pair of ordinary brass scales, with a set
of troy weights, I paid, on behalf of the party, fifteen
dollars, the seller consoling me by the information
that in his opinion, if the gold-hunters continued to
pour in for a fortnight longer, I would not have got
the article for three times the amount.

Furnished with my purchase, I returned to the
tent, and the stock of gold dust realised by each man
was weighed, and computed at the current rate in
which the mercantile transactions of this little colony
are reckoned—namely, fourteen dollars each ounce of
gold dust. We found that M'Phail and Malcolm had
been, upon the whole, the most successful, each
having obtained nearly two ounces of pure gold
dust, valued at twenty-eight dollars. I myself had
about twenty-three dollars' worth, and Bradley had
twenty-five dollars' worth. An amount which, considerable though it was, we hope greatly to increase
as soon as we get our cradle into operation.

During the day, there were numerous arrivals
from Sutter's Fort ; and in my opinion, these diggings will soon be overcrowded. Two of the new-
comers were known to Bradley—one, a Mr. Biggs, a

shipping agent from San Francisco ; the other, Mr. Lacosse, a French Canadian, who has recently settled in California. They accepted our offer for them to join our party. If this influx of people continues, I think the Yankee with the store will do better than any one ; and keeping a shanty will be a far more profitable speculation than handling a shovel or working a cradle. What surprises me is, that in this remote spot, so distant from anything that can be called Law, so much tranquillity prevails under the circumstances. One hears of no deeds of violence, or even dishonesty. In fact, theft would hardly pay. The risk would be more than the advantage : for if any one was detected plundering, he would soon have a rifle-bullet put through him. One thing in favour of good order is, that here there is no unequal distribution of property—no favoured classes. Every man who has a spade or a trowel, and hands to use them, is upon an equality, and can make a fortune with a rapidity hitherto almost unknown in the history of the world.

Sunday, June 11*th*.—Nearly a week has elapsed since I last opened my diary. On Tuesday, we set to work upon our cradle. We resolved upon the con- struction of two ; and for this purpose, went down to

the store in a body, to see about the boards. We
found the timber extravagantly dear, being asked
forty dollars a-hundred. After some bargaining, we
obtained sufficient for our purpose, at the rate of
thirty-five dollars.

The next question was, as to whether we should
hire a carpenter. We were told there were one or
two in the diggings who might be hired, though at a
very extravagant rate. Accordingly, Bradley and I
proceeded to see one of these gentlemen, and found
him washing away with a hollow log and a willow-
branch sieve. He offered to help us at the rate of
thirty-five dollars a-day, we finding provisions and
tools, and could not be brought to charge less. We
thought this by far too extravagant, and left him,
determined to undertake the work ourselves. Meantime, Horry had brought down two of our horses
with him to the store. We loaded them immediately with boards, and returned to our tent.

After breakfast, which consisted of coffee without
milk, flour cakes, and strips of dried beef, roasted on
the embers, we set to work. We had a sufficient
number of axes and a good stout saw, one large plane,
and a few strong chisels, with plenty of nails. As

may be expected, we proved to be very awkward
carpenters. Mr. Lacosse was perhaps the handiest, and
Malcolm not much inferior to him, until the latter
unfortunately received a severe cut with a chisel,
extending in a transverse line along the joint of the
fore-finger of the left hand. I strapped up the wound,
but the rough work soon tore away the diaculum :
no bad consequences, however, ensued. The wound,
in spite of the hard treatment which it received, closed
and healed by the first intention—proving the healthy
habit of body engendered by temperance and constant
exercise in the open air.

In building our cradles, or " gold canoes," as the
Indians called them, we found that to mortice the
planks into each other was a feat of carpentering far
above our skill, particularly as we had no mortice
chisels. We were therefore obliged to adopt the
ruder experiment of making the boards overlap each
other by about an inch, nailing them firmly together
in that position. As, however, the inequality of surface at the bottom of the cradle, produced by the mode
of building, would have materially impeded our operations, we strained some pieces of tarred canvas, which
we fortunately possessed amongst our tent cloths, over

the bottoms, thus rendering the surface even, and suited to our purpose. By the time we had got so far with our undertaking, we felt sufficiently tired to give over work for the night. We had laboured unceasingly at them, pausing only to swallow a hasty meal, and stuck by our hammers and chisels till dusk. We were up early the next morning, and toiled away to get the cradles completed, as we were constantly seeing proofs of the great advantages of these machines. We fixed a wicker sieve over the head, by means of a couple of transverse bars, and then set about to construct the working apparatus, which we had all along feared would put our mechanical skill to rather a severe test; but we found it easier than we had anticipated, and before sundown the rockers were fixed on both cradles, which, to all intents and purposes, were now ready for us. The work was rather rough, but it was firm and strong. So fearful were we first of all that our cradles might be removed or tampered with in the night, that I jocularly proposed two of us should give up the shelter of the tent, and, like pretty little children, sleep in our cradles till the morning.

The next day we set to work with them with the

utmost eagerness, having first dragged the lumbering machines to a likely spot in the vicinity of the water. The labour was hard enough, but nothing compared to the old plan of pot-washing, while it saved the hands from the injury inflicted by continual dabbling in sand and water. We took the different departments of labour by turns, and found that the change, by bringing into play different sets of muscles, greatly relieved us, and enabled us to keep the stones rolling with great energy. In the evening, with the help of our newly purchased scales, we tested our gains. The cradle which was worked by Don Luis, Malcolm, and myself, for it was so near the water that three hands were sufficient, had realised six ounces of gold dust ; the other, attended to by Bradley, M'Phail, Biggs, and Lacosse, had nearly as much. During the day there was another considerable influx of people to the diggings ; the banks of the river are therefore getting more and more crowded, and we hear that the price of every article of subsistence is rising in the same proportion.

CHAPTER XI.

The proceedings of the week—Visit from Mr. Larkin—What will the Govern
ment do?—What " enough" is—San Francisco—Houses and ships deserted
—A captain and ship without a crew—A ship without a crew or captain—
Wages, newspapers, and shovels—The Attorney-General to the King of
the Sandwich Islands—Something for the lawyers—Gold-diggers by moon-
light—Mr. Larkin's departure—Provisions run short—Seek a supply at
Salter's—Good luck—Diggings' law—Provisions arrive—A wagon wanted
— Arrival of Californians and their families—Gay dresses and coquettish
manners—Fandangos—El Jarabe—The waltz—Lookers-on and dancers—
Coffee, and something stronger—No more Sunday work—José and the
saints—The Virgin Mary cheated—Contemplated migration.

June 18*th, Sunday*.—The proceedings of the past week
have been but a repetition of those of the week previous, the amount of gold dust realised being rather
greater, and amounting on an average to very nearly
sixteen ounces per day. Cradles are now in use every-
where around us; nevertheless, the numbers who stand
in the water washing with tin or wooden bowls do not
appear to be diminished.

On the evening of Thursday we were visited by a
gentleman from Monterey, a Mr. Larkin, who, I
believe, is connected with the States Government, and
who has arrived in the diggings with the view of

making a report to the authorities at Washington. Don Luis immediately recognised him, and invited him to spend the evening and night in our tent. We were very anxious to hear the news from the coast, and Mr. Larkin in turn was very anxious to pick up all the information he could get respecting the diggings. Don Luis says he is a man of large fortune, so his tour is purely one of inspection, and not with any eye to business. We made him as comfortable as we could ; Lacosse exerted himself in the manufacture of the coffee in honour of our guest, and we had several hours of interesting conversation.

Mr. Larkin said he had no idea what steps the Government at Washington would take with reference to the " placer." " It can't matter much to you, gentlemen," observed he, " for although there can be no doubt of its being upon public territory, still, before any instructions can be received from Washington, the great body of the diggers and washers here will be enriched to their heart's content, if a man ever does feel contented with any amount of wealth."—" Your observation," exclaimed Malcolm, " puts me in mind of a story which my father used to tell of a farmer, a friend of his, who once took his rent, the odd money

E

short, to an old miserly landlord rolling in wealth.   He
was asked by him why he had not brought the full
amount.   ' Why,' replied the farmer, ' I thought you
had enough.'—' Enough !' said the miser ; 'do you
know what *enough* is ?   I 'll tell you—Enough is
something more than a man hath !' "

Mr. Larkin then spoke of the effects of the
" mineral yellow fever," as he called it, having been
most extraordinary in San Francisco.   When he left
that town, he said more than two-thirds of the houses
were deserted.   We were not surprised at this, as we
knew the people who were continually arriving here
must have come from somewhere.   Nearly all the
ships in the harbour too had lost a great part of their
crews by desertion.   A barque called the Amity had
only six men left when Mr. Larkin started from the port.
On board another ship from the Sandwich Islands the
captain was left actually and literally alone.   On the
road Mr. Larkin fell in with another captain who had
started off for the gold region with every man of his
crew, leaving his ship unprotected in port.   On Mr.
Larkin remonstrating with him on the flagrancy of
his conduct, he merely replied, " Oh, I warrant me
her cables and anchors are strong enough to last till

we get back " Mr Larkin told us what we were fully prepared to hear, namely, that wages and salaries of all classes have risen immensely: clerks, he said, were getting from nine hundred to twelve hundred dollars, instead of from four hundred to five hundred and fifty dollars, with their board. Both the *Star* and *Californian* newspapers, he said, had stopped. Thinking to surprise us, he told us that shovels which used to be one dollar were selling in San Francisco, when he left, for five and six dollars each. Bradley replied that he thought this was a very reasonable figure, for he had heard thirty dollars offered for a spade that very day.

" Do you know, by-the-bye," said Mr. Larkin, " who I saw here to-day, up to his knees in water, washing away in a tin pan ? Why, a lawyer who was the Attorney-General to the King of the Sandwich Islands, not eighteen months ago."—" I guess," said Bradley, " he finds gold-washing more profitable than Sandwich Island law ; but he 's not the only one of his brethren that is of much the same spirit; there 's lots of lawyers in these diggings. Well! they are better employed now than ever they were in their lives. They 're money-getting rascals all the world over;

but here they do have to *work* for it, that's one
comfort." Before turning in, we took a stroll through
the camp with Mr. Larkin. It was a bright moon-
light night, and some of the more eager diggers
were still at work. These were the new-comers,
probably, who were too much excited to sleep without trying their hands at washing the golden
gravel. Mr. Larkin left us the following day.

June 23rd, Friday.—The last entry in my diary
seems to have been written last Sunday. Next day
we began to find the provisions running short. A
consultation was accordingly held upon the subject.
It was quite out of the question to buy provisions in
the diggings. Work as one might, the day's living
of any man with a respectable appetite—and one
seems always to feel hungry here—would pretty well
absorb the day's labour. We therefore determined to
dispatch Bradley and José back to Sutter's Fort for
a supply, it being stipulated that Bradley should share
in the gold we might find during their absence.
This arrangement being duly concluded, they started
off the following morning on horseback, driving
before them the two beasts we purchased at Sutter's.
We instructed Bradley, if possible, to buy a light

wagon, in which to store the provisions he was to
bring back. The two extra horses would be able to
draw it, and such a vehicle would be useful in many
respects. He took with him two hundred and fifty
dollars' worth of gold, so as to be in sufficient funds,
in case the sum demanded should be an over-exorbi-
tant one.

They departed on Tuesday, and we continued our
labours. Towards the afternoon of that day, I had
a piece of great good luck. I was digging up the
earth to throw into the cradle, when I turned up a
lump of ore about the size of a small walnut, which
I knew at once was a piece of gold. It weighed two
ounces and three-quarters. This, by the law of the
diggings—for it is curious how soon a set of rude
regulations sprung into existence, which everybody
seemed to abide by—belonged to myself and not to
the party, it being found before the earth was thrown
into the cradle, and being over half-an-ounce in
weight. Higher up the Sacramento, and particularly on Bear River, one of its tributaries, these
lumps and flakes were said to be frequently met
with ; but at the Mormon digging they are very
rare.

On Thursday, about sundown, we were delighted
to see the approach of Bradley with a well-loaded
wagon of light but strong construction. He had
just arrived in time, for our larder was almost
exhausted. We were prepared, however, to have
stood out another day or two on short rations, rather
than pay the prices asked at the shanties. Bradley
gave us a short account of the expedition. They
reached Sutter's in safety, and found the Fort as busy
as though it was tenanted by a swarm of bees. A
sort of hotel had at last been opened, and the landlord was driving a roaring trade. The emigrants
were pouring in, purchasing shovels, trowels, pans,
and whatever else they wanted, at high prices. Profitable as was the washing business, Bradley said he
suspected the store-keepers at the Fort were clearing
more by their branch of the enterprise than if they
had their hands in the pan themselves. He found
Captain Sutter well and hearty, and, the morning
after his arrival, consulted him about a wagon. The
Captain, however, had none he felt inclined to sell,
nor was there such a thing to be got in the fort.
After some consideration, however, Captain Sutter
said that Mr. Sinclair, whose rancho was about three

miles off, on the opposite bank of the river, might
be able to accommodate him.   Accordingly, Bradley
made the best of his way there, but found Mr.
Sinclair indisposed to trade.   At length, after a good
deal of persuasion, Bradley succeeded in hiring a wagon
and a wagoner of him for a week.   The vehicle was
got across the river that night.   In the morning he
started it off well laden with provisions, and arrived
here without any accident the same evening.   We
were now well victualled for a month, but were
puzzled how to stow away our large stock of provisions, and only accomplished it satisfactorily by
giving up the tent for this purpose.   This compelled
us all to sleep in the open air ; but as yet the nights
are very mild and pleasant.

Among the fresh arrivals at the diggings the native
Californians have begun to appear in tolerable numbers.
Many of these people have brought their wives, who
are attended usually by Indian girls.   The graceful
Spanish costume of the new-comers adds quite a
feature to the busy scene around.   There, working
amidst the sallow Yankees, with their wide white
trowsers and straw hats, and the half naked Indian,
may be seen the native-born Californian, with his

dusky visage and lustrous black eye, clad in the universal short tight jacket with its lace adornments, and velvet breeches with a silk sash fastened round his waist, splashing away with his gay deer-skin botas in the mudded water.

The appearance of the women is graceful and coquettish. Their petticoats, short enough to display in most instances a well-turned ankle, are richly laced and embroidered, and striped and flounced with gaudy colours, of which scarlet seems to have the preference. Their tresses hang in luxuriant plaits down their backs; and in all the little accessories of dress, such as earrings, necklaces, &c., the costume is very rich. Its distinguishing feature, however, is the reboso, a sort of scarf, generally made of cotton, which answers to the mantilla of Old Spain. It is worn in many different and very graceful fashions—sometimes twined round the waist and shoulders; at others, hanging in pretty festoons about the figure, but always disposed with that indescribable degree of coquettish grace which Spanish women have been for ages allowed to possess in the management of the fan and the mantilla. Since these arrivals, almost every evening a fandango is got up on the green, before some of the tents. The term fandango, though originally signifying a peculiar kind of dance, seems to be used here for an evening's dancing entertainment, in which many different *pas* are introduced.   I was present at a fandango a few nights ago, where a couple of performers were dancing "el jarabe," which seemed to consist chiefly of a series of monotonous toe and heel movements on the ground. The motions of the foot were, however, wonderfully rapid, and always in exact time to the music.   But at these entertainments the waltz seems to be the standing dish.   It is danced with numerous very intricate figures, to which, however, all the Californians appear quite *au fait*.   Men and women alike waltz beautifully, with an easy, graceful, swinging motion.

It is quite a treat, after a hard day's work, to go at nightfall to one of these fandangos.   The merry notes of the guitar and the violin announce them to all comers; and a motley enough looking crowd, every member of which is puffing away at a cigar, forms an applauding circle round the dancers, who smoke like the rest. One cannot help being struck by the picturesque costumes and graceful motions of the performers, who appear to dance not only with their legs, but with all their hearts and souls.   Lacosse is a particular

E 3

admirer of these fandangos, and he very frequently takes
a part in them himself. During the interval between
the dances, coffee is consumed by the senoras, and coffee
with something stronger by the senors ; so that, as the
night advances, the merriment gets, if not " fast and
furious," at least animated and imposing.

25th June, Sunday.—We have all of us given
over working on Sundays, as we found the toil on
six successive days quite hard enough. Last week we
had rather indifferent success, having realized only
nineteen ounces of gold, barely three ounces a man.
The dust is weighed out and distributed every evening, and each man carries his portion about his
person. José, who has amassed a tolerable quantity
by working in his spare time, is constantly feeling
to see whether his stock is safe. He weighs it two
or three times a-day, to ascertain, I suppose, whether
it exhausts itself by insensible perspiration, or other
means, and invokes, by turns, every saint in the
calendar—his patron-saint, Joseph, in particular—
and all his old heathenish Spirits, to keep his treasure
safe. In accordance with a vow he made before he
started from Monterey, he has set apart one-fourth
of his treasure for the Big Woman, as he calls

the Virgin Mary—in contradistinction to the Great Spirit, I imagine ; but I fancy her stock of gold decreases every day, and that José does n't play her fair.

We had a great deal of serious conversation this afternoon upon the propriety of moving farther up the river, and trying some of the higher washings ; for our last week's labour was a terribly poor yield. We remembered Captain Sutter's account of how Mr. Marshall had first discovered the gold in the vicinity of his mill, and how plentiful it seemed to lie there. Besides, the diggings are getting over-crowded ; the consequence of which is, that we have had several of our pans and baskets stolen. We therefore decided that, if we could sell our cradles to advantage—and there is some likelihood of this, for there is not a carpenter left all through these diggings to make others for the constant new comers—to move higher up the Fork, and try our fortune at a less crowded spot. There is one thing that I think I shall regret leaving myself, and that is, the fandango and the two or three pretty senoritas one has been in the habit of meeting at it almost every night.

CHAPTER XII.

The party leave the Mormon diggings—Cradles sold by auction—Laughter and
biddings—The wagon sent back—The route to the saw-mills—A horse in
danger—A miss at a Koyott—An antelope hit—Mr. Marshall—Venison stakes
for supper—The saw-mills—Indians at work—Acorn bread—Where the gold
was—How it was got—Gentlemen and horses—New-comers—"Yankee
Doodle" and the " Star-spangled Banner."

Sunday, July 2nd.—Yesterday, in accordance with
the resolutions debated this day week, we left the
Mormon diggings, and pursued our course up the
Americans' River. It was on Thursday night that we
adopted the final determination of moving off from
our late quarters ; and, accordingly, next day I walked
with Bradley and M'Phail through the diggings, to
try to find purchasers for our cradles. This was not a
difficult task. We had plenty of offers ; and we were
so importuned by some six or eight people, who were
anxious to trade with us, that we decided in a minute
on having an auction of them. I was not bold enough
to play the part of auctioneer myself, but Bradley very
coolly mounted on the top of one of the machines, and

called upon "gentlemen traders" for their biddings. This
was a capital move. The highest offer we had previously
obtained was one hundred and sixty dollars for the largest
of the two machines; but Bradley succeeded in coaxing
the purchasers on—stopping now and then to expatiate
on the mint of gold, which, he guessed, he would
warrant it to produce daily; and then calling to their
minds the fact that this was " the identical cradle into
which the lump of gold weighing two ounces and
three-quarters—the largest piece ever found at the
Mormon diggings—was about to have been shovelled
when it was discovered and seized hold of by the fortunate digger—the gentleman on my right hand—who, as
you all know, in accordance with the admirable laws of
these diggings, laid claim to it as his private property."
This produced a roar of laughter; but, what was
better, it produced a roar of biddings, and the cradle
was knocked down at one hundred and ninety-five
dollars, payable in gold dust, at the standard rate of
fourteen dollars the ounce, or a discount of ten per
cent. if settled in broad silver pieces. The other cradle
fetched us one hundred and eighty dollars.

For these two cradles, therefore, we got three
hundred and seventy-five dollars' worth of dust. The

same night we occupied ourselves in constructing strong bags, made of rough hides, and well strapped round the person, for the conveyance of the gold dust and scales which we had already amassed.

On Wednesday morning, before sunrise, we had sent the wagon and wagoner back to Mr. Sinclair's rancho, accompanied by José, who returned on the evening of Thursday with the horses.

We found, on starting, that our horses could not carry all the provisions, and at the same time perform a good day's work. We, therefore, left some of the more bulky articles under the charge of a man from San Francisco, known to Bradley, and departed. We made good progress for a mile or two; and, as we crossed the brow of a hill, halted a moment to observe the busy aspect of the washings, as they appeared from a distance. The country, as we ascended the stream, became hourly more hilly and broken. Its general aspect was grassy, and the soil appeared fertile. Here and there deep gullies crossed our path, over which we had great difficulty in urging the horses, heavily loaded as they were. At one of these ravines, the animal which conveyed the tent-poles lost his footing, and went scrambling down the edge of the descent, bearing with him a whole avalanche of gravel and shingles. Malcolm and Lacosse went after the brute, and succeeded in forcing it up by a less precipitous path.

At noon we halted and dined. During the afternoon, we observed a sort of small jackall, of the kind called Koyott, hovering about the line of march. It only occasionally showed itself amongst the long rank grass and bushes. Bradley, however, got his rifle ready, but, although he fired several shots, the animal was too nimble or restless for even the practised eye and hand of a Yankee rifleman to be certain of his aim. In a shot at a young antelope which bounded past, however, Bradley was more successful; and we were rejoiced at the prospect of a supper on tender venison. In a few minutes he had slung the animal over his horse's haunches, and we proceeded on our route.

The country became more broken and mountainous as we advanced; and in approaching the location of the saw-mills, the hills appeared to rise nearly one thousand feet above the level of the Sacramento. They were diversified by groves of gigantic pine and oak trees. We were looking anxiously about for the saw-mills, when we heard the crack of a rifle; and presently a man in white linen trowsers, with his legs defended by buckskin mocassins, wearing a broad Mexican sombrero, and carrying his rifle in his hand, approached us. This person turned out to be Mr. Marshall. He received us kindly, and asked the news from the lower washings, and also how matters were looking at Sutter's when we passed through. Mr. Marshall had a gang of fifty Indians employed, and Captain Sutter had another party of nearly double that number, on the same bank of the river.

We encamped in a woody bottom, by the side of a small stream, which joined the main torrent here, and where there was good pasture for the horses. Mr. Marshall's house was about a mile and a half further up the river. After a good supper of vension stakes —thanks to Bradley's rifle—we turned in for the night.

Next day, Lacosse and M'Phail, attended by Horry, and driving two extra horses, rode down to the Mormon diggings, for the purpose of getting up the provisions which we had left behind. Meantime, I walked out to reconnoitre our new quarters. I soon arrived at the mills, and saw the spot where the discovery of the gold had first been made, by the torrent laying bare the sides of the mill-race. Here I met Mr. Marshall again. Of course the operations of the saw-mill had been stopped, for the workmen were employed in the vicinity, either above or below the works, digging and washing on their own account. Mr. Marshall paid the Indians he had at work chiefly in merchandize. I saw a portion of the gang, the men dressed for the most part in cotton drawers and mocassins, leaving the upper part of the body naked. They worked with the same implements as those used in the lower washings. Not far from the place where most of them were employed, I saw a number of the women and children pounding acorns in a hollow block of wood with an oblong stone. Of the acorn flour thus produced, they make a sort of dry, hard, unpalatable bread, which assuredly none but an Indian stomach could digest.

Upon instituting a more particular search into the nature of the country and our prospects, we found that the places where the gold was found in the greatest abundance, and in the largest masses, were the beds of the mountain torrents, now dry, which occasionally descend into both the forks of the stream.

We clambered up some of those precipitous ravines, and observed, upon several occasions, as we scrambled amongst the shingle, shining spangles of gold. The soil was evidently richly charged, but the great disadvantage was the comparative distance from water. In the evening our friends arrived from the lower diggings, with the provisions all safe and sound, and next day we determined to set to work.

July 3rd.—Selecting a likely place in the heart of a steep mountain gorge, we transported thither the larger Indian baskets which we had purchased at Sutter's Fort, and, shovelling the earth into them, passed poles, cut from the nearest pine tree, through the rope-handles we had affixed to these baskets. Resting the poles on our shoulders, we carried the loaded baskets to the brink of the stream, and then set to work after the old fashion, with our hands in the baskets. Our success was great, and the day's return shows a decided improvement upon the Mormon diggings. The soil here is more richly impregnated with gold than below; but the labour of carrying the earth to the water is excessive, and I am so tired this evening that I very reluctantly opened my journal to make this short entry.

July 4th.—As we were starting off to the river with our first basket loads of gravel this morning, Lacosse suddenly remarked that he did not see why the horses should be living like gentlemen when the gentlemen were working like horses; and he proposed to use the shoulders of our nags, instead of our own, for the conveyance of the earth. We all fell in with this proposal, wondering it had never struck us before, and the horses were soon fetched from their comfortable quarters among the tall rank grass, and set to work, with the baskets slung over their backs, like panniers.

Several new-comers from the Mormon diggings passed us to-day, bound further up the Fork. In the morning Mr. Marshall paid us a visit, to know how we were getting on. He had heard from Captain Sutter, who stated that he thought of starting for the upper or lower washings himself, as soon as he had gathered in his wheat harvest, which he hoped to accomplish during the present week. A number of wild ducks haunt the river, and especially abound in the grassy and weedy pools which skirt its edges. This morning we shot some of these, and found them an agreeable addition to our dinner bill of fare.

The afternoon has been passed among the greater part of the miners here as a celebration of the anniversary of American Independence.   Something like an out-door feast was got up, and toasts were drank and songs sung; "Yankee Doodle," and the "Star-spangled Banner," being the chief favourites.   Bradley made a smart speech; and, contrary to his usual practice, complimented us Englishmen with a round of pleasant allusions to the mother country.

CHAPTER XIII.

The party again shift their quarters—The river forded—Horry in the water—
Mr. Sinclair's party of Indians—Deserted Indian villages—Weber's Creek—
A halt made—Cradles hollowed out—A commotion in the camp—Colonel
Mason arrives on a tour of inspection—His opinions as to what Congress
should do—Military deserters, and what ought to be done with them—
Return of Colonel Mason's party to Sutter's Fort—Bradley accompanies it
with a stock of gold—How the gold was packed, and what precautions
were taken for its security.

WEBER'S CREEK.

July 9th.—A few more days' experience at the
saw-mills convinced us that much time and labour
was lost in consequence of the distance between the
digging we worked at and the water, and we therefore
determined to seek a more desirable location. Ever
since we had been at the saw-mills we had heard it constantly said, that at Weber's Creek the gold was to
be found in far greater abundance; and to Weber's
Creek we determined to go. The stream thus called
is a small tributary to the northern fork of the
Americans'.

We struck our tents yesterday morning, loaded
our horses, and took our departure. The river, at the

fording place, was broad and rapid, but shallow; the
principal difficulties in the ford arose from the number
of smooth round stones, covered with green rince
slime, which formed the bed of the river, and over
which our horses stumbled, with a violence which
threatened to disturb the fastening of their burdens.
No disaster, however, actually occurred, except to
poor Horry, whose horse stumbled over a large
boulder, and pitched its luckless rider over its head
into the water, to the undissembled delight of the
entire party, who hailed the poor sailor's discomfiture
with loud bursts of laughter. Horry made the best
of his way to the further bank, without paying any
more attention to his horse, which, however, emerged
from the water, and was on dry land as soon as
Horry himself.

We now proceeded along the right bank of the
North Fork, and on the opposite side we caught a
glimpse of a party of Indians at work, which we
afterwards learned to be that of Mr. Sinclair. In one
week this party had gathered sixteen pounds troy of
fine washed gold dust. They worked hard, were well
fed, and had liberal rations of "strong water" daily.
We rested a couple of hours at noon, in a pleasant

bottom, heavily timbered, and afterwards, striking away from the river at an acute angle, moved leisurely on through a broken country, intersected by many water-courses, and overgrown with dense clusters of trees.

During our afternoon march we passed several deserted Indian villages—the round-shaped skeletons of the huts alone remaining to mark the former settlements. Not a member of the tribe, however, was to be seen; the beaver may build and the deer pasture hereabouts in peace. Towards evening we entered the valley drained by the stream called Weber's Creek. Its appearance was very beautiful, and the stream descended along a steep rocky bed, foaming round large boulder stones, and tumbling down low ledges of granite. The grassy slopes of the valley are cut up in all directions with rivulets, the courses of which are marked by luxuriant underwood, rank grass, and groves of stunted oaks. Two or three arbours were to be seen with one or two rude-looking tents, all with blazing fires before them. We encamped forthwith, hoping the next day to reach a station which we could make available for our purpose.

We were early on the move this morning, and soon saw several parties of threes and fours washing in the bed of the river, or exploring the mountain gorges with their shovels and mattocks. The weather was getting oppressively hot; indeed, the further we got from the Sacramento the hotter did it become. The sea-breeze never penetrates here to refresh us, and, except when an occasional squall comes sweeping down from the hills, the air is very oppressive.

We travelled but slowly, still in an hour or so we reached a station, about fifteen miles as the crow flies, or about twenty by the windings of the stream, from the point of its junction with the Americanos, where we determined to try our luck. There was quite a camp here—not to the same extent as the Mormon diggings, but still the washers were numerous, and the larger part of them were Indians. Some few worked in the bed of the river, but the great majority were engaged in the ravines leading up the mountains. The greatest quantity of gold dust was found in the former, while the latter yielded the best specimens of lump and scale gold. We were told that, though the side gullies were very rich, yet they were more uncertain than the main stream

Lumps of gold, weighing several ounces, were continually met with, but a morning was often wasted and nothing found ; whereas, if a man stuck to the main stream, and washed all day long, he was sure of his ounce or couple of ounces of gold. For these reasons we determined to stand by the river. Our first business was to see if we could manage to construct a couple of cradles. At a large store here we met with some pine planks, but the figure was most exorbitant. Taking a hint from what we had noticed among the Indians at the saw-mills, we determined to fell a couple of stout trees, and hollow them out so as to serve our purpose. We obtained the assistance of a man here, a ship's carpenter, and a most civil obliging sort of fellow, who gave us a day's help for thirty dollars. He superintended the felling of the trees, and then put us in the way of proceeding with the work. We found the toil sufficiently severe, and began to feel the heat, as I thought, to a far greater extent than was the case in the lower part of the country.

July 8*th*.—Yesterday we were employed, from early in the morning till beyond noon, in trimming and hollowing out our cradles. While we were seated

F

together outside the tent enjoying a few whiffs of our
pipes and cigars, after a famous dinner of smoking-hot
steaks and frijoles, we saw the camp below was all
in commotion. People were running out of their
tents, and shouting to their neighbours, and gradually
a little crowd was formed round a group of horsemen,
who were just then brought to a halt. That same
feeling of curiosity which gets together a London
crowd to see the lion on the top of Northumberland
House wag his tail, caused us to make our way, with
the rest of the gapers, down to Bennett's shanty,
against which all this bustle appeared to be going on.
As soon as Bradley and myself could force our way
a little through the crowd, we recognised in a moment
the features of Colonel Mason. The Colonel, who
wore an undress military uniform, had just dismounted from his horse, with the intention, it appeared, of walking through the diggings. In a
couple of minutes' time my friend Lieutenant Sherman came up, and we were soon engaged in an
animated conversation in reference to the gold district. The fact was, the Governor was on a tour of
inspection for the purpose of making a report to the
Cabinet at Washington. I took care to thank Lieu-

tenant Sherman for his letter of introduction to Captain Sutter, and to explain to him the friendly manner in which Captain Sutter received me. I then joined in the conversation being carried on with Colonel Mason, who was giving his opinion as to what the Government would do with respect to the gold placer. The Colonel was very guarded in his statements. He, however, hinted that he thought it would be politic for Congress to send over proper officers and workmen, and at once to establish a mint at some convenient point on the coast. He fully admitted the difficulties of keeping men to their engagements under circumstances like the present ; but said some steps must be taken to check the system of desertions on the part of the troops quartered at Monterey and San Francisco. The pay of the soldiers, he considered, ought to be increased ; but, without reference to this, he told the gentlemen round him that, as good citizens, they were bound to lend their utmost endeavours to secure in safe custody all known deserters—men who had abandoned their flag and exposed the country to danger, that they might live in a state of drunkenness at the mines.

Colonel Mason next proceeded to visit Captain

Weber's store, whither Bradley accompanied him. On
his return, Bradley informed us that the Colonel and his
escort intended to set off on their way back to Sutter's
Fort that very afternoon, and they reckoned upon
encamping some few miles below the saw-mills that
night. Bradley then took me aside and asked me
whether this would not be a good opportunity to
send our stock of gold dust down to Captain Sutter,
who would, for a reasonable commission, consign it to
a merchant at Monterey on our account. The weight
of it was becoming cumbersome, and we were besides
in constant apprehension of some unfortunate accident
happening to it. Now was the time, Bradley urged, to
place all we had as yet realised in security. He knew
Colonel Mason—in fact, had served under him, and
undertook, if the remainder of the party were agreeable,
to carry the gold, under the protection of Colonel
Mason's escort, to Sutter's Fort.

There was something reasonable in this proposal,
and Colonel Mason, on being appealed to, said he
would gladly give Mr. Bradley such protection as his
escort would afford him, and would be, moreover,
happy of his company. Our party was, therefore,
summoned together, and the whole, or nearly so, of

the gold dust being produced, it was weighed in our presence, and found to amount to twenty-seven pounds eight ounces troy—valued at over four thousand six hundred dollars.   Bradley gave a regular receipt for this to the company, and engaged to obtain a similar one from Captain Sutter.   The gold dust was then packed in a small portmanteau well secured by numerous cords, and firmly bound on the pack-saddle of an extra horse, which Bradley was to ride alongside of, the bridle of the animal being secured to his arm, and its trail-rope made fast to the saddle of the horse which Bradley himself rode.   He was well armed with pistols and a rifle, and started with Colonel Mason's party a couple of hours before sun-down—so that they might ford the river ere it was dusk.   After accomplishing this, they intended to ride part of the way by the light of the moon.

CHAPTER XIV.

Smoking and sleeping—Fever, and how caused—Bradley returns—A doctor
wanted—A doctor's fee at the mines—Medicine scarce—A hot air bath
and a cold water bath—Indians engaged to work—Indian thimble-rigging
—An Indian gamester, and the stake he plays for—More sickness—Mormons move off—A drunken dance by Indians—An Indian song about the
yellow earth and the fleet rifle—An immodest dance by Indian women.

July 12th, Wednesday.—We finished our cradles
late upon Saturday night, but delayed working until
Monday. A few of the miners pursued their avocation
on the Sunday, but the majority devoted the day to
rest—smoking and sleeping in the shade alternately.
I walked through the washings, and heard that many
of the miners had been taken ill with intermittent
fever, a circumstance which did not astonish me. Bad
diet, daily exposure to the sun while it is at its greatest
height, followed by an exposure to the cold damp air
at night time—these conjoined were quite sufficient to
bring on the most severe illness. On my return to the
tent I looked over our little stock of medicine, which
I foresaw I should soon be required to use.

On Monday we commenced operations in the old

style—digging, fetching water, and rocking the cradle. The sun came blazing down with great power, causing headaches to most of the party, particularly Malcolm, who complained much. The day's taking was very good; we having realised nine ounces with one machine, and seven and a half with the other. At night, as Malcolm still continued to complain of his head, and as there was evidently a good deal of low fever about him, I gave him a dose of calomel and a febrifuge mixture, which by the morning produced a good deal of relief.

Bradley made his appearance during the forenoon, after a fatiguing ride from Sutter's Fort. He had seen the Captain, had delivered the gold, and settled the transaction. We were hard at work the whole of to-day. In the evening a man came crawling into the tent to know if we had any medicines we would sell. I told him I was a doctor, and asked him what was the matter. He had been suffering from remittent fever of a low typhoid type. I gave him bark, and told him he must lay up and take care of himself. He said he would; but next day, during the intervals of fever, I saw him working away with his pan. The news of there being a doctor in the camp soon spread, and I

am now being continually called on to prescribe for a
large number of patients. An ounce of gold is the fee
generally given me. This sort of work is as much more
profitable as it is less laborious than working at the
cradle. But the great drawback is that one has to
do something else beyond advising. People require
physicking, and as I cannot submit to be deprived of
the little stock of medicine I had brought with me
in case of my own friends having occasion for it, I am
obliged to give over practising in those cases where
medicine is absolutely necessary.

The native Californians, both Indians and whites,
have an universal remedy for febrile affections, and
indeed for sickness of almost any kind ; this is the
temascal, a sort of hot air bath, shaped not unlike a
sentry-box, and built of wicker-work, and afterwards
plastered with mud until it becomes air-tight. There
is one of these machines at the Weber Creek washings,
which has been run up by the Indians during the
last few days. One of them used it for the first time
this afternoon, and to my surprise is still alive. After
a great fire had been made up close to the door—a
narrow aperture just large enough for a little man
to squeeze through—it was afterwards gradually

allowed to burn itself out, having in the meantime
heated to a very high degree the air in the interior of
the bath. Into this the Indian screwed himself, and
there remained until a profuse perspiration was produced, which he checked forthwith by a plunge into
the chilly water of the river. Here he floundered
about for a few minutes, and then crawled out and lay
down exhausted on the ground.

The atmosphere continues exceedingly sultry, and
the miners who work by the river, out of the shade,
have in several instances sunk exhausted under the
toil. Dysentery, produced probably by unwholesome
food, has also begun to show itself, and altogether the
aspect of things is anything but cheerful.

July 15th, Saturday.—We have engaged a large
party of Indians to work for us in the ravines. They
belong to the Snake tribe, and appear to be a poor set
of half-starved wretches. We pay them in provisions,
and occasionally drams of pisco—a spirit made from
Californian grapes.

On visiting the encampment of our Indians, last
night after work was over, I found about a dozen of
them eagerly engaged gambling away—the stake, in
some instances, being the supper which had just been

served out to them—with an ardour equal to that of the most civilized gamesters. So far as I could make out, the game had some analogy to our "thimble-rigging;" but appeared to be fairly played. A small ball was passed by three of the Indians from hand to hand, with such rapid dexterity, that no eye could keep pace with their movements; three others watched it with peculiar eagerness. Every now and then the latter made a correct guess, and one was scored in their favour—if wrong, a mark was scored against them. The Indians are in general strongly addicted to games of chance, and they sometimes gamble away all the clothing on their backs. I heard of an instance which occurred near the saw-mills, of an Indian who, after having lost every article of clothing he had, one after the other, to his more fortunate antagonist, staked his labour for a week against the cotton shirt which he had lost only a few minutes before. He had a run of bad luck, and when he left off, had to work for six weeks, at gold-washing, for his antagonist, who fed him on nothing better than acorn bread. Mr. Neligh, who told me of this circumstance, had seen the man at work duly fulfilling his engagement.

The sickness amongst the miners continues to

increase, and in our own party Lacosse has been laid
up for two days with fever; however, I think he is
now doing well.   The climate does not appear to be
unhealthy.   It is the exposure to the work which does
the mischief.   There is some talk afloat among our
party of removing further up the country, nearer to
the mountains, where gold is said to be in greater
abundance.   Yesterday, a large party—many of them
Mormons—started for the Bear River, a small stream
which runs into the Sacramento, and is said to be
about fifty miles distant, due north from where we
are encamped.

The Indians at work here have caused the price
of pisco and whisky to rise to a most exorbitantly high
rate.   They content themselves with feasting on the
bitter acorn bread, and spend all their earnings on
" strong water" and a little finery.   Sometimes a party
of them, when intoxicated, will get up one of their
wild dances, when the stamping and yelling are of a
far more fearful character than is generally the case at
these singular exhibitions.   The dance begins generally with a rude song, the words being of the usual
harsh guttural character, but the ideas are generally
striking and peculiar.   One has been explained to me

which recites the praises of the "yellow earth," because it will procure the Shoshonee the fleet rifle with which he can slay his Pawnee foe.   It says nothing, however, about the "strong water," which renders the arm of the war-chief weaker than that of a child; for, with all their vices, there is still that pride about the Indian character which makes them ashamed of those weaknesses they are unable to resist.

Frequently, while the Indian warriors repose from their exertions, after the termination of one of these wild dances, the women of the tribe will occupy their place; but in general their postures and movements are indelicate in the extreme.   But modesty is hardly to be looked for in the amusements of savage life.

CHAPTER XV.

Monday, July 24*th.*—We have determined to start for the Bear River. We worked hard last week, but suffered greatly from the heat; almost every man of us complains of feverish symptoms, with pains in the limbs, back, and loins, yet we are better than the majority of the miners. These washings have now become nearly as crowded as the Mormon diggings were when we left them, and immense sums have been made by some of the luckier adventurers amongst the ravines. The whole valley is dotted over with tents and green bush arbours, and there is hardly a water-course but which is sprinkled with miners, digging, sifting, and washing. About half of the people work together in companies—the other half shift each for himself.   There are hundreds of Indians, many of them fantastically dressed, for they can purchase fine clothing now, even at the extravagant rates at which all articles are charged at Weber's store. They labour one day, and get drunk on pisco or the " strong water" on another.   One of them rolled down a rocky ravine lately, in an intoxicated state, and was killed.

As we were lying down in the shade of the tent yesterday, we were visited by an old trapper called Joe White.   He had recognised Bradley and Don Luis, whom he had met on the coast, and we invited him to take coffee with us.   Joe White had come into this part of the country with Captain Sutter, whom he spoke very highly of, and of whose early efforts to form a settlement he gave us an account. Their party was the very first of the white settlers in the wilderness.   They lived some time in a camp formed of the tented wagons they had brought with them, until they could run up a few rough shanties, and some protecting outworks.   During the time they were constructing these, and indeed for some months afterwards, they were dreadfully harassed by the Indians, who made onslaughts on their cattle, carried away, killed, and eat both horses and oxen. The Indians are by no means particular. One night, after the party had been lulled into a sense of security by the apparent friendly disposition of the Indians, who occasionally came into their camp, and no watch was being kept, upwards of a score of horses and mules were driven off; the loss of which Sutter's people knew nothing of until they woke up in the morning, and found the ropes all cut. They started off at once on the trail, and soon found that it led to an Indian rancheria, about eight miles up the Sacramento. This rancheria was, they believed, the refuge of the "Ingin varmints," as Joe White styled them, from whose depredations they were constantly suffering. Captain Sutter determined to take signal revenge. They returned to the Fort that day, but next morning started of in a strong party, each man armed with his never-failing rifle and big bowie-knife, and taking with them a howitzer which the Captain had brought with him over the Rocky Mountains. The Indians must, however, have had information by their scouts of the expedition ; for, when the party reached the rancheria, they found it deserted—not

even a solitary squaw left among the huddled-up
collection of huts. Determined not to be foiled, the
party set to work to demolish the village. The construction of the Indian houses rendered this an easy
task, but, to complete it, fire was requisite. No
sooner had the smoke risen from the kindling wood,
than their ears were saluted with a dismal yell from
a little densely-wooded island a couple of hundred
yards up the stream. Starting out in all directions
from the high grass and underwood, appeared a
crowd of squaws with their children, who gave
whoop after whoop, and, brandishing boughs of
trees, imprecated curses upon the destroyers of their
rancheria.

Captain Sutter and his party of trappers were
somewhat startled at this proceeding, and the question
immediately occurred to them as to where the men
could be. The party pushed their way homewards as
fast as possible, leaving the rancheria burning and the
squaws and children still yelling and whooping on
the island. It was as they expected. On coming
within two miles of the Fort, they heard the crack
upon crack of distant rifles. Putting their horses to
the gallop, they arrived just in time to see the Indians

totally routed, and scampering away as fast as their horses would carry them into the woods.

After this double defeat, the tribes seem to have given up all idea of prosecuting a war against their new neighbours, and, gradually relinquishing their thievish habits, settled in the neighbourhood of the Fort—sometimes hunting and trapping for the pale faces, and at others labouring away at ditching and brick-making, being paid chiefly in articles of clothing and small allowances of pisco. The trapper told us that Captain Sutter has now a tin coin in circulation, stamped with his name, and good for a certain amount of merchandize at the Fort.

After listening to a few more wonderful adventures of this sort, Bradley turned the conversation upon the country about Bear River. The trapper said he knew it well, and had heard that there was plenty of gold there. He asked him if he would undertake to guide us thither, and, after some bargaining, he consented. The sum he was to have was sixty-five dollars and his food. Considering the high rates of all things here, this was a low figure enough, but the old trapper candidly told us that he was sick and tired of paddling about in the water washing for gold, and

that he would prefer a few days' jaunt in the wilderness. The climate was much cooler further to the
north, he informed us, and comparatively few miners
had penetrated to the Bear Valley. We had a long
debate upon the matter, and ultimately it was determined to start the day after to-morrow (Wednesday).

July 25th, Tuesday.—This day has been devoted
to preparations for our journey. Our stock of provisions, with the exception of breadstuffs, are quite
exhausted. We have had, therefore, to lay in a stock,
but we found everything, of course, inordinately dear;
so we have contented ourselves with buying some
bacon, and dried beef, and coffee, resolving to trust
to our rifles for further support, there being plenty of
game in the neighbourhood of the Bear Valley. By
the advice of Joe White, we intend not only to load
the pack-horses with a portion of our stock of provisions, but each man is to take a fortnight's rations
for himself. The pack-horses will carry about another
fortnight's supply. We should have preferred, if we
could have managed it, to despatch the gold we
have amassed since Bradley's mission to Captain Sutter, down to the Fort ; but, after some deliberation,
we have resolved not to risk its transit without an

escort, and, accordingly, have agreed to load one horse, the most sure-footed of the lot, with the valuable burden, and to attach its trail-ropes to the horses ridden by ourselves in turn.

This evening three men, hearing of our intended expedition, offered to join the party. These were Edward Story, an American lawyer who had been one of the inferior alcaldes during the Spanish regime at Monterey; John Dowling, first mate, and Samuel Bradshaw, the carpenter, of an American whaling ship which they had left at San Francisco. The lawyer was an intelligent person, conversant with the language of several of the tribes—the mate seemed to have his wits about him, and the carpenter would obviously be a great acquisition, particularly as we were now about to plunge even beyond the furthest outposts of civilization, where, in all probability, we may have to secure ourselves against attacks from the Indians without the possibility of any help beyond that which we could render to each other. We were rather pleased with their offer, and received them as an addition to our party. All three had horses, although, as usual with seamen, the mate and carpenter were terribly awkward equestrians.

Wednesday, July 26th.—This day we struck our camp before sunrise, and had the horses securely packed and all in motion in the early cool of the morning. The march was a fatiguing one ; the country appearing to be a succession of woody bottoms, or valleys and steep rocky ridges, which tried the metal of our loaded horses severely. From the summit of one of the hills more elevated than the rest we obtained a distant view of the valley of the Sacramento. Our general course was north north-west. The trapper, who proved an able guide, varied the direction from time to time so as to lead us through the easiest paths, taking care to steer clear of the deep canones that split up the hills in every direction. We dined at noon as usual, and that very well, on some hare soup made from a couple of hares which we had shot during the morning, and some dried beef. The signs of deer were very frequent. After mounting and descending a very precipitous and rocky ridge, we encamped near some waterfalls in a wide open valley. The night was somewhat cold, and we enjoyed a blazing fire of pine sticks, which we cut from the dried trees in the vicinity.

Friday, July 28th.—Yesterday morning dawned

clear and rather coolish. In the forenoon we crossed
the north fork of the Americanos, which was here but
a trifling stream. The general character of the country was becoming more and more mountainous and
difficult to traverse, and we found the labour of the
journey sufficiently severe. A great number of water-
courses crossed our path, but the channels were quite
dry, the stones and shingle white and bleaching in the
sun. An unfortunate accident occurred during the
afternoon's march to one of the pack-horses, which
stumbled over a heap of rough stones in clambering up
from the bed of a torrent, and broke its leg. We had
to shoot the poor animal to put it out of pain. Its
burden was equally distributed between its more fortunate fellows. We encamped amongst rocks, and had
a poor supper of flour cakes and bacon scraps. During
the night Don Luis was attacked with aguish symptoms. I prescribed bark, which appeared to relieve
him.

To-day our horses were quickly saddled and
packed, and we started off in the faint grey of the
morning. It was chilly, but the sky was beautifully
clear. When the sun had fairly risen, however, we
had no more cold to complain of. The way was

exceedingly difficult. We toiled along precipitous ravines and gullies, and climbed up steep and rocky ridges, which cut and wounded the feet of the horses, and rendered our progress very slow. The timber we passed was principally pine trees, with sharp pointed leaves and large cones, and occasionally we came upon a grove of evergreen oaks, more stunted in shape than was the case in the lower regions. About mid-day we passed the source of the Rio de las Plumas, or Feather River, and after a most severe and in some respects forced march climbed the last rocky ridge which separated us from the Bear Valley. The sun was near its setting as we pushed down the mountain slopes towards the river. We found it a small stream flowing swiftly over a shingly bed to the westward, and encamped within hearing of its murmur, well pleased to have performed our toilsome journey.

CHAPTER XVI.

A rest—A solitude—No gold to be found—An exploring party—Good fortune—
Food and security—More cradles—A fortified shanty in preparation—A
dessert after dinner—Dejection—Thoughts about home—No other gold-
finders to be seen—Mormon trail—Salt Plain and the Great Salt Lake—A
weary day's journey without water—Saline exhalations—The inland sea and
its desolate shores—A terrible whirlpool—The shanty finished—The trapper's services retained—The camp visited by an Indian tribe—A friendly
sign—The pipe of peace—A "trade" with the Indians declined—Some
depart and some remain—Provisions run short—Hunting expeditions—
Something about a bear.

Sunday, July 30*th.*—We rested somewhat late upon
Saturday morning to make up for the fatigues of the
journey from Weber's Creek. On surveying the
country we found ourselves in a perfect solitude. Not
an Indian, far less a white man, was to be seen. The
fertile valley of the Bear River—with its luxuriant
grass, in which nestled coveys of the Californian quail
—seemed almost untrodden by human foot, and sloped
in great beauty between the ridges of rocky hills and
peaks of granite, with dark ravines and canones between, which hemmed it in. Our first care was of course
to try the capabilities of the country in the way of
gold. We therefore separated ourselves, and sought

different points of the channel of the stream, and
different chasms, which in the winter time conducted
the mountain torrents into it.

To our great astonishment and disappointment, one
by one we returned into the camp with the news of
our non-success.   By the old trapper's advice, an
exploring party was despatched to followup the stream
towards its head.   They travelled the distance of some
ten or twelve miles, crossing some of the more important tributaries of the main river, and had the good
fortune to strike upon a spot where a slight examination was sufficient to prove that the gold existed in
great abundance in the sand and shingles, and
imbedded in flakes amid the rocks.   To-day
we have moved the camp to this spot ; and, as
we are now beyond the reach of aid from white
men, and have begun to feel that we must be, for
some time at least, a self-supporting party, our first
thoughts are turned towards making arrangements for
obtaining a supply of food, and for ensuring our
security.   Bradley, Joe White, and José, are to be
our hunters ; Malcolm, Lacosse, and M'Phail, are to
set to work to-morrow to make a couple of cradles,
the carpenter giving them an occasional helping hand,

but occupying himself principally in superintending the construction of a large shanty, sufficient to accommodate the whole party, with a rough fortification around, composed of pine logs and palisades, pointed at the top, sufficient to enclose a space of ground into which the horses could be driven at night, out of the way of any outlying Indian who might be thievishly inclined. We calculate that the construction of the shanty, with its appurtenances, will occupy at least a week—in all probability, much longer. Malcolm, M'Phail, and Lacosse, are to join us in our labours as soon as they have finished the cradles. The hunters had good luck to-day, and came in with a couple of fat bucks. The trapper had also snared a number of quails, so that our table was nobly furnished. Our dinner, also, included a dessert of a fruit similar to apples in taste, but not larger than well-grown gooseberries. These had been gathered and brought in by the trapper.

Sunday, August 6th.—I have felt very low-spirited these last few days. One's thoughts have turned towards home, and an indescribable sensation of melancholy has been weighing me down, which at last my companions have begun to take notice of. This even-

ing, just as the remainder of the party contemplated
turning in for the night, I pulled out my note-book,
and began writing beside the camp-fire.

" ¿ No puede Vm. dormir ?" said Don Luis to me,
as he moved away towards the tent.

" No, Senor," replied I.   " Pienso a la veja Ingle-
terra; a mi Hermano y a mis amigos."

" Por ventura a una amiguita," observed Don Luis.

I laughed, and answering, " Es possible, Senor,"
went on writing.

We are now regularly settled on the Bear
River, and have, as yet, seen no signs of human
life round about us.   The reports, therefore, which
we heard at Weber's Creek of the gold-finders
having penetrated into this valley, would appear
to have been without foundation.   We have observed
a fresh-made trail, which the old trapper seems
to consider passes in the direction of the Truckee
Lake; and we have noticed the remains of several
camp-fires at different parts of the valley.   In all
probability, this trail has been made by the Mormon
emigrants, who are reported to have gone on a gold-
hunting expedition across the salt desert to the shores
of the Great Salt Lake, a distance of seven or eight

hundred miles.   The old trapper had some wonderful
stories to tell about the dangers of the journey across
the Salt Plain.   How that a man has to travel, from
the first faint break of grey light in the morning, as
hard as his horse will carry him, over a desert of
white salt—which crunches and crumbles beneath his
horse's tread at every step he takes—until the sun has
gone down behind the tall peaks of the distant Sierra
Nevada.   No water but of the most brackish kind can
be procured to refresh either horse or rider through
the whole of this weary route, while their lips are
parched with thirst, and their eyes and nostrils become
choked from the effects of the saline exhalations rising
up on all sides from the desert over which they are
passing.   And as for the Great Salt Lake, the desolate shores of this inland sea have been, for the most
part, carefully avoided by both Indians and trappers,
and no living being has yet been found daring enough
to venture far on the bosom of its dark, turbid waters ;
for a belief exists that a terrible whirlpool agitates
their surface, ready to swallow up everything that may
venture within the bounds of its dangerous influence.

Our cradles were finished on Monday, and the
shanty on Saturday afternoon.   It includes a sort of

outhouse for cooking, and the rude palisades around are quite sufficient protection for the horses against any attempts the Indians are likely to make to drive them off. As soon as our building labours were over yesterday, we set to work digging and washing, and were very successful. The country about here is of course much more rugged than in the lower diggings. Grass is plentiful in the valley, but the rocky heights are covered with a stinted vegetation, offering no food to our horses. The soil, mineralogically considered, does not seem to vary materially from that in the neighbourhood of Weber's Creek. If anything, it is more impregnated with gold. On Friday, Don Luis discovered a large rough lump in a cañon about a mile from the shanty ; and the next evening a similar lump, though rather smaller, was picked up by Bradley in one of his hunting excursions.

August 8th.—We have engaged the services of our friend the trapper at the rate of fifteen dollars a-week, with an allowance of whisky twice a-day. He will hunt for us, but will have nothing to do with gold digging and washing. He has a tolerable contempt for dollars, or else he would have demanded higher wages. A man who has spent nearly all his

life in the wilderness, who has known no wants but
such as his rifle could quickly supply, may, however,
well look with contempt on the "root of all evil." If
he were hungry, a shot at some panting elk or bellowing buffalo would stock him with food for weeks to
come. If he were athirst, the clear water of some
sparkling rivulet would yield him all that he would
require. The hide of the bear or of the buffalo would
serve to clothe him and to shelter him from the sharp
night frosts; while a score of beaver skins would purchase him ammunition more than sufficient to last him
all the year round. What, then, should he want with
gold?

Yesterday, while we were at dinner, we were
surprised by seeing a party of Indians approaching the
camp from the direction of Truckee Lake. They
appeared not to have any hostile intentions, so we
quietly awaited their approach. The foremost chief
held before him a long stick, with a bunch of white
feathers dangling at the end. Story explained to us
that this was a friendly sign, and said we had nothing
to fear from the party. As they approached nearer
towards us, they commenced dancing and singing, and
we could soon perceive that very few among them

were armed, and that altogether their appearance was
anything but warlike and imposing.

Story went out to meet them, and shook hands
with the few foremost chiefs.   When they reached
the shanty, before the door of which we were seated,
the chiefs gathered on the right-hand side of us, and
squatted themselves down upon the ground, when
the pipe of peace was immediately produced by a
veteran chief, and handed round.   I took a few
whiffs with the rest, and then we learnt from our
visiters that they were anxious to engage in a trade.
All that they had, however, were some few esculent
roots and several bags of pine-nuts.   These last they
roast and eat, but the taste is far from pleasant.   In
exchange for them they wanted some charges of
powder and ball.   Three of them, I noticed, possessed
old Spanish muskets, of which they seemed particularly proud ; they held them in the usual cautious
Indian style, with the butt-end clutched in the right
hand, and the barrel resting on the left arm.   A few
of the others had bows and arrows slung across
their backs.   We pleaded shortness of ammunition as
our excuse for declining the trade.   Our provisions
being run low made it impossible for us to offer them

anything to eat, so we gave them a few blankets, which we could well spare, by way of keeping ourselves in their good graces; as, according to Story, they would have considered it a great affront if we had neglected to make them any presents.

The Indians remained and encamped outside our fort; last night, and this morning the greater part took their departure. The guard last night had orders to keep a sharp look-out, as we thought that our friends, even though they had no hostile intentions towards us, might still take a strong liking to some of our horses ; but nothing of a suspicious character occurred. Five young men of the tribe also have stopt behind, who wish to continue with us and work for us, but the low state of our commissariat renders it desirable not to accept their offer, unless our hunters return to-day with a good stock of provisions.

August 13*th.* Our hunters have been very successful these last few days. We have a large stock of elk meat, which we intend drying after the Indian fashion. On Friday, while Don Luis and the trapper were out together, they were surprised by the sight of a huge bear right before them, slowly walking up towards them. As soon as he arrived within about a hundred paces he squatted down upon his haunches for a few moments ; but, as they got nearer to him, and just as they were preparing to give him a greeting in the shape of a couple of balls through his head, he rose up and scampered off. They fired, but without success, and the brute plunged into a dense thicket; after which they saw nothing more of him.

Our Indians, after stopping with us a couple of days, during which period we compelled them to encamp at night-time outside the fort, took their departure early on Friday morning, or else during the night of Thursday, unperceived by our sentinels. They, however, took nothing with them belonging to our party, except a couple of blankets we had lent to the two principal men.

CHAPTER XVII.

A rich mine of gold discovered—A guard both night and day—A good morning's work—An Indian scout—How he served Dowling, and how Dowling
served him—A look-out—Indians seen advancing—A moment of fear—A
yell—Arrows and rifles—A wounded chief carried off—The field of battle—
The return to the camp—Horses driven off by Indians—Where Jose was
found—The wounded attended to—An after-dinner discussion—How the
watch went to sleep, and how they were woke up—M'Phail missing—
Wolves, deer, and a puma—A party set out in search of M'Phail.

August 20*th, Sunday.*—The past week has been in
many respects an eventful one. On Friday, while
several of us were rambling about the neighbourhood
of the camp, exploring the numerous mountain canones which lie between us and the Sierra Nevada, we
found, among the loose particles of rock which had
crumbled away from the sides of the ravine and fallen
to the bottom, several lumps of gold of a much larger
size than any we had before met with. This induced
us to examine the upper part of the ravine, where
promising traces of gold were readily detected ; further
examination convinced us that the precious metal
existed here in far greater quantities than in the locality

where we had been at work for several weeks previous ;
and we were, moreover, satisfied that it was to be
obtained with much less difficulty. As being found in
solid lumps, the unpleasant labour of washing was dis-
pensed with.   We therefore determined, on the following morning, to remove all our implements to this spot,
the only disadvantage of which was its being situated
rather far off from our place of encampment.

Since our friends, the Indians, had quitted us, we
had always left some one or other on guard at the
shanty, to keep watch over our horses and baggage,
both during the day time and at night ; for we knew
that some of them were continually prowling about, our
horses having frequently shown signs of uneasiness in
the night time.   During the day there was generally
one member of the party who remained at the shanty,
having either José or the lad Horry in company.

The ravine we proposed moving to was nearly
half-a-mile distant.   After breakfast, Bradley, Lacosse,
and M‘Phail, accompanied by the old trapper, set off
on a hunting expedition, for our stock of provisions
was now getting very low, leaving José and our legal
friend at the camp.   The remainder of the party,
including myself, proceeded to the ravine with our

implements, and after working a few hours we succeeded in procuring more gold than we had obtained
in any two days during the past week. We were
just on the point of returning to the camp to dinner
when Dowling, who was standing near some sage
bushes at the upper part of the ravine, heard a rustling
among them, and on moving in the direction of the
noise saw an Indian stealthily creeping along, who, as
soon as he perceived he was discovered, discharged an
arrow, which just missed its mark, but lacerated, and
that rather severely, Dowling's ear.   The savage
immediately set up a most terrific whoop, and ran off,
but stumbled before he could draw another arrow from
his quiver, while Dowling, rushing forward, buried his
mattock in the head of his fallen foe, killing him
instantaneously.

At this moment we heard the crack of a rifle in
the direction of the camp, which, with the Indian's
whoop at the same moment, completely bewildered us.
Every man, however, seized his rifle, and Dowling,
hastening towards us, told us of what had just occurred.
All was still for the next few moments, and I mounted
a little hill to reconnoitre.   Suddenly I saw a troop of
Indians, the foremost of them on horseback, approach-

ing at full speed. I hastily returned to my companions, and we sought shelter in a little dell, determined to await there, and resist the attack, for it was evident that the savages' intentions were anything but pacific.

It was a moment of breathless excitement. We heard the tramp, tramp of the horses coming on towards us, but as yet they and their riders were concealed from our view. I confess I trembled violently, not exactly with fear, although I expected that a few moments would see us all scalped by our savage assailants. It was the suddenness of the danger which startled me, and made my heart throb violently; but at that moment, just as I was reproaching myself with the want of courage, a terrific yell rung through the air at a short distance from us, and forty or fifty warlike Indians appeared in sight. My whole frame was nerved in an instant, and when a shower of arrows flew amongst us, I was the first man to answer it with a rifle-shot, which brought one of the foremost Indians off his horse to the ground. I instantly reloaded, but in the meanwhile the rifles of my companions had been doing good service. We had taken up our position behind a row of willow trees which skirted the banks of a narrow stream, and here we were protected in a great measure from the arrows of our assailants, which were in most cases turned aside by the branches. A second volley of rifle-shots soon followed the first; and while we were reloading, and the smoke had slightly cleared away, I could see that we had spread consternation in the ranks of the Indian warriors, and that they were gathering up their wounded preparatory to retreating. I had my eye on one old man, who had just leapt from his horse. My finger was on the trigger, when I saw him coolly advance, and, taking one of his wounded companions, who had been shot through the leg, in his arms, place him on a horse, then mounting his own, and catching hold of the other animal's bridle, gallop off at full speed. Although I knew full well that if the fortune of the day had gone against us, these savages would not have spared a single man of our party, still I could not find it in my heart to fire on the old chief, and he carried off his wounded comrade in safety.

In a few minutes the hill-sides were clear, and when we emerged from our shelter, all that was visible of the troop of warriors was three of them weltering in their blood, a bow or two, and some empty quivers, and a few scattered feathers and tomahawks, lying on

the ground.   One by one, we gradually stole up to
the top of the mound from whence I first beheld the
approach of the enemy, when, finding that they were
retreating at full speed in an opposite direction to the
camp, we determined to proceed thither at once, fully
prepared to find both Story and José murdered.   On
our arrival, however, the former coolly advanced to
meet us, and, in answer to our questions, stated that
while he was superintending the proper browning of
our venison, and José was filling the cans with water,
he saw several of our horses scampering off, being in
fact driven by three or four Indians on horseback.
" So quickly," said he, " was the movement effected,
that before I could lay hold of my rifle they were
nearly beyond range. I fired, but without effect; and
while I was looking about, I suppose in rather a
bewildered manner, a party of something like forty
Indians ran rapidly past.   I don't know whether
they saw me or not, but I was by no means anxious
to engage their attention, and was glad enough when
the last passed out of sight.   I then went in search of
José, whom I found in the river up to his neck in
water—a position which he thought afforded the safest
means of concealment, as he knew his wild brethren

would have sacrificed him, and perhaps eaten him forthwith, if they had chanced to discover him."

I at once set to work to dress Dowling's ear, and a wound which Don Luis had received in his hand. The latter was merely a scratch, and the only danger likely to arise from it was in the event of the arrow by which it was inflicted having been poisoned. But Don Luis felt so confident that this was not the practice among the tribes about here, that he would not allow me to take the usual precautions against such a contingency.

Our anxiety was now turned towards the party who were out hunting, and we anxiously looked for their appearance. We had been so upset by the events of the morning, that we all felt disinclined to resume our labours after our meal was concluded, and we occupied ourselves in and about the camp, and in discussing the reason of the Indians' attack, and the probability of its being followed up by another. The day wore on without any signs of our companions' return. Towards evening, a rifle was fired off occasionally, to let them know of the danger which in all probability awaited them from an attack on the part of the Indians, and also to let the latter gentry

know that we were on the look-out.   It was arranged
that we should all keep watch until the arrival of our
friends, to be the better prepared for any danger
which menaced us and them ; for we thought it not
unlikely that the Indians were hovering about the
camp, and might attempt a surprise. Exhausted,
however, by excitement and fatigue, one by one we
dropped off to sleep.   I was wakened up by the
report, as I thought, of a rifle, which was immediately
followed by a horrible moaning, and the whole of us
were soon on our legs, rifles in hand, in the expectation of being butchered in the course of a few minutes.
Bradley's well-known whistle, however, somewhat
restored our confidence.

In a few minutes Lacosse, Bradley, and the old
trapper were by the camp-fire. "Is M'Phail here?"
asked all of them in a breath, anxiously looking round
the circle.   The reply to the question was a sad one :
he had not yet returned.   In answer to our inquiries
as to where they had parted from him, and as to
whether they had heard the rifle-shot which had disturbed us from our sleep, Lacosse replied that they
had first missed him about three-quarters of an hour
ago, but they did not feel any particular uneasiness at

the circumstance, as they imagined he had ridden on
first. The night was rather dark, but Lacosse said
the trail could easily be distinguished. With regard to
the shot we had heard fired, and the moans which
followed it, Bra dley aid, that shortly after missing
M'Phail they found some wolves were on their track,
in all likelihood scenting the deer which they were
carrying slung across their horses. Fearing their
noise might attract a more dangerous customer, in the
shape of a puma, towards them, he fired a couple of
pistols, which had the effect of wounding two of the
pack, who rolled over with terrific howls. It must
have been Bradley's last shot that woke us, for none of
us heard more than one shot fired.

Our three huntsmen set about preparing their
supper immediately, in the full expectation that
M'Phail would make his appearance before the venison
was ready. The supper was, however, cooked and
eaten, but still no M'Phail arrived. Another hour was
suffered to elapse, and then we began to consider that
it was nearly three hours ago since he was last seen,
while at that time he was not more than one hour's
distance from the camp. It was evident, therefore,
that he had either missed the trail or followed it in

the opposite direction (which last was the old trapper's opinion), or else some more serious misfortune had happened to him. We at once resolved to set out in search of him, leaving a guard behind at the camp. The mate and Don Luis, being both, as it were, invalided, were of course among those who were to remain. Bradley pleaded fatigue, and wished to stay in camp, and Biggs was left on guard with him.

CHAPTER XVIII.

IT must have been about one o'clock when we
started, and, after half-an-hour's hard riding, we came
upon the spot where M'Phail had last been seen. We
shouted for some time as loudly as our lungs would
let us, but heard nothing, save the howl of some
hungry wolf, in reply. We then followed the trail
at a brisk pace for eight or nine miles, but could
discover nothing of our missing friend. There seemed
no possibility of ascertaining whether he had proceeded in the direction in question or not, as the
marks made by the horses of the party in the morning,
on their way out, somewhat confused the old trapper.
His keen eye, however, soon detected marks of a

horse's hoof in a contrary direction, over the marks
which the horses of the hunting party had made on
their return.   These signs were not apparent beyond
the spot we had reached.   In which direction they
were continued, the night was too dark to discover.

Feeling that further search before daybreak would
be useless, we resolved to get a few hours' sleep in
the meantime ; and, dismounting from our horses,
secured them as well as we could, and placing
our saddles on the ground, to serve as pillows, we
wrapped our saddle-cloths round us, and were soon
fast asleep.   Story and the lad Horry did first duty
as sentinels.   While they were on guard I was
wakened by a sharp tug at my leg, and while I
was seizing hold of my rifle, I recognised Story's voice
calling me by name.   He told me that, after keeping
a sharp look-out for about half-an-hour, he observed
several fires on the hill-sides, apparently about half-
a-mile off ; he had been watching them for some
time, and at last determined to wake one of the
party.

I went with him outside the little willow copse
where we had fixed ourselves, and true enough there
were the fires, belonging, as we thought, to a camp

of Indians—very likely the same who had stolen our horses and attacked us in the morning. We returned and woke the whole party ; and, a consultation being held, it was decided, as we were well armed, and as the Indians had shown so much anxiety this morning to get beyond reach of our weapons, after tasting a few shots, to effect a surprise, and recover, if possible, our stolen horses. We saddled and mounted as quickly as possible, and, after riding about a mile in the direction of the fires, found that we were getting tolerably close to our enemies. On we went, taking every bush which crackled beneath our horses' tread for a token of the movements of some Indian scout who had scented our approach. When within a short distance of the camp-fires we dismounted, and tied our horses to some trees, leaving them in charge of the lad Horry, with directions for him to keep his ears well open, and, in the event of his hearing us retreat from the Indians, to give a few lusty shouts, so as to let us know where the means of flight were to be found.

We advanced cautiously, Malcolm and Bradshaw preceding the main body, about twenty paces apart. The arrangement was for the five (namely, Lacosse,

Story, the Trapper, José, and myself) who composed
the main body to form a semicircle, of which the
two scouts would compose the extreme points, and
so to approach the Indians' camp, on nearing which
we were to fire a volley on them from our rifles, and,
wheeling round, drive our horses off and retreat.
We were within two hundred paces of the camp-fires
when we were startled by the report of a rifle.   A
shrill whistle followed, but we still advanced, and in a
few moments came up with Malcolm and Bradshaw,
the sailor being supported in the arms of his com-
panion, who called out that the man was shot, and
begged me to look to him.   The remainder of the
party, hearing this, moved a few paces forward, levelled
their rifles, and were on the eve of firing, when we
were suddenly saluted, in true British vernacular, with
an exclamation of " D—— your eyes, who goes
there ?"   This so startled our party that it saved the
lives, very probably, of the whole camp.   They halted
for a moment, and consulted together as to the course
to be adopted.   A shot had been fired from
the camp, and one of our men injured.   They,
therefore, concluded that we had stumbled on
the camp of one of those gangs of ruffians which were

known to infest the hills at the foot of the Sierra Nevada.

At this juncture I ran up to the group with the intelligence that Bradshaw had been injured by a shot from his own rifle, which had accidentally gone off, and which circumstance Malcolm had not, in the first instance, explained. I told my companions that the man was wounded seriously in the leg ; that I had merely bandaged it up with a handkerchief, and, leaving him in Malcolm's charge, had hastened forward to let them know the fact, that no more blood might be shed. No sooner was this explanation given than we heard a loud shout from the lad Horry, followed, as I thought, by some faint groans ; but none of the others heard them, and I thought I might have been mistaken. It was concluded that he was merely shouting in accordance with our instructions, and no further notice was taken of the affair. At that instant several horses came galloping by at full speed, passing within a few yards of us, and, following them, we could discern half-a-dozen mounted Indians. We guessed the truth at once. They had cut the bridles of our horses, and were driving them away to rejoin their fellows,

which had been stolen from us in the morning.
We levelled our rifles and fired—reloaded, and fired
again ; and then, in the midst of a chorus of hallooing and screaming from the camp just before us,
and the loud bellowing of the retreating Indians,
started off in pursuit, and soon succeeded in turning
our animals round, the Indians vanishing as rapidly
as they had appeared.

Securing our steeds, we walked them back in the
direction of the spot where we had left Horry, and,
after some trouble, succeeded in finding the exact
place, when, to our horror, we found the poor fellow
quite dead, his body covered with blood, and his head
and face dreadfully disfigured. A closer examination
showed us that the poor lad, after being murdered,
had been scalped by the savages. " Yes, yes," said
the old trapper, " sure enough his scalp is dangling
in the belt of one of them devils. G-d! I 'll send
an ounce of lead through the first red-skin I meet
outside them clearings. We 'll have vengeance—we
will."

As soon as I was a little recovered from the horror
which this scene naturally caused, I returned with the
old trapper to the spot where I had left Malcolm and

Bradshaw, hardly expecting, after what I had just witnessed, to find either of them alive. I was, however, happy in my fears not being realized. They were both as I had left them. We carried the wounded man as well as we could between us back to the place where the remainder of the party were waiting for us. Here we stayed till daybreak, silent and dejected. For my own part I could have wept. That rough sailor lad, though under other circumstances I might have looked down on him with contempt, and not have cared one straw whether he was dead or alive, had been one of a little society, every member of which had grown upon me in the rude life we had lived together in this wilderness, and I felt that I had lost a friend.

The day broke at last, and after repairing our bridles as well as we could, we prepared to depart. We wrapped the body of the dead lad in a blanket, and laid it over the back of his horse to convey it to our camp, where we might bury it according to the rites of the English church. I examined the carpenter's leg, and found his hurt was, fortunately, only a flesh wound. It gave him, nevertheless, great pain to travel on horseback, but there was no other

H

means of conveying him to the camp. As we rode slowly along, in the grey light of the morning, we caught sight of the valley, the scene of our last night's misfortunes, and saw on the hill-sides two white-tented emigrant wagons, with the horses quietly grazing down in the bottom. Several of us rode towards the spot, but found not a soul there. One of last night's mysteries was explained. The camp we had at first taken to be an Indian one, and then one of mountain robbers, was merely that of a few emigrants, who, having crossed the pass in the Sierra Nevada, were, doubtless, on their way to the Sacramento Valley. In all probability, alarmed by the extraordinary affair of last night, they had abandoned their wagons, and sought concealment from the dangers which they imagined surrounded them. We shouted out the words "Friends," "Americans," and other expressions, to give them confidence, if they were within hearing, but we obtained no reply. We, therefore, hastened to rejoin the remainder of our party, and in about three hours' time we reached the camp, cheering ourselves with the thought, as we moved along, that we should find M'Phail had returned. But we were doomed to disappointment;

there were no tidings of him, and sorrowfully did we set to work to dig poor Horry's grave. After Malcolm had read the service from the English Prayer-book over him, we sawed off a pine-log, which was inserted a couple of feet deep in the ground, and on the upper part, which had been smoothed for that purpose, we carved, in rude letters, his name, and the date of his death.

CHAPTER XIX.

The party strengthen their defences—No tidings of M'Phail—The trapper
goes in search of him—Returns, having met with no success—M'Phail
makes his appearance accompanied by guides—His adventures while
away—Finds he is lost—Loses his rifle—No supper—Loses his horse—No
food for three days—Sinks into a stupor—Is discovered by two Indians
Their humane treatment of him—They conduct him by slow marches to the
camp.

August 27*th*.—We have passed a heavy, but not
very profitable week. Three days of our time have
been spent in strengthening our defences, and we
have had some severe labour in felling pine trees and
dragging them to the stockade. We have driven
sharpened stakes into the earth, and, after laying
the logs longitudinally within them, have twisted the
lighter boughs and brush-wood of the trees in the
interstices. Before we began this task, however, the
trapper, Malcolm, and Lacosse started in search of
M'Phail, but returned the same night (Sunday)
unsuccessful. In the meantime, my two patients got
on favourably ; the pure air and temperate living doing
more for the wounds than medical skill could effect.

On Monday, a council was held as to the propriety of sending another party in search of our missing friend ; and, after some discussion, the trapper started off alone, taking rations with him to last him two or three days. On Wednesday we set to work again, digging and washing, confining ourselves, however, to that portion of the stream and to those canones which were in the vicinity of the camp. Upon the whole, we made good progress during the week, frequently averaging four ounces of gold dust and flakes a day per man. Early on Wednesday the trapper made his appearance, but he had returned without any tidings of our missing friend.

It was upon Thursday evening, as we were returning to the camp after a hard day's work, that we were delighted at perceiving our comrade M'Phail, whom we had given up for lost, making his way towards us, accompanied by a couple of Indians, fantastically dressed in the Spanish fashion, the costumes having been probably purchased by the sale of gold dust lower down the country. Our friend was, of course, joyfully received, and a special can of pisco punch brewed in honour of his return.

His adventures since his separation from the party

were soon related.   He had turned aside to water his
horse at a small rivulet, and, on his return, waited
at the trail for his comrades, whom he conceived to
be still in the rear.   After waiting for nearly half-
an-hour, he thought that they must have passed him,
and galloped after them in what he conceived to be
the proper trail.   After half-an-hour's ride, however,
he found himself utterly at sea—no sign of the camp,
or of his comrades.   He mounted several high ridges,
which he hoped might command a view of the Bear
Valley ; but all he could see was a wilderness of hills
and deep ravines, here and there chequered with fertile
bottoms clumped with pines and oaks.   In fact, he
grew quite confused, and, to add to his perplexity,
in fording a rapid torrent his horse stumbled, and was
carried off his legs by the strength of the stream,
and had to swim for it.   At length they gained the
further bank ; but our friend found that in his agitation
he had dropped his rifle, which was irrecoverably
gone.

Finding that he had no knowledge of the country
about him, he determined to encamp for the night, and
accordingly laid his head on his saddle, wrapped himself up in his cloak, and went supperless to sleep.

When he awoke in the morning, he found that his horse, which he had tethered to a neighbouring stunted tree, had strayed away, and although he followed his trail for some time, he was eventually obliged to give up the search. The remainder of this and the following day he wandered about at random, amidst a wild and sterile country, furrowed with tremendous chasms several hundred feet in depth, and the edge of which it was necessary to skirt for miles ere a crossing-place could be found. During this time poor M'Phail fared very hardly. He saw numerous herds of elk, but they bounded past unharmed : he had no rifle. He tried in vain to find some edible roots, and was at length reduced to the necessity of chewing grass and the pith of alder trees.

Throughout this period his sufferings were excessive ; but as the time passed and brought no relief, he experienced a sickness and nausea of the most gnawing and horrible description. He became so weak that he could hardly stand. At length at sunset, on the third day of his wanderings, he laid himself down upon a spot of grass, and fell into a kind of stupor, in the full belief that he would only wake in the agonies of death. It was then that he was discovered by the

two Indians who brought him to the camp. They
behaved with great humanity towards him, allowing
him, however, to eat, first of all, only a few morsels
of the dried meat which they had with them, that
he might not harm himself by over-eating, after such
a lengthened fast. As his stomach by degrees recovered its tone, they permitted him to take further
nutriment; and after encamping with them on that
and the following night, he felt sufficiently recovered
to proceed on his journey to the camp. His kind
benefactors understood a few words of Spanish, and
he was enabled to explain to them the part of the
country he wished to reach. They undertook to guide
him thither—told him they would arrive there after
having slept once, and by slow marches made their
way to Bear Valley, which they reached on the evening of the second day. M'Phail expressed his surprise
on finding that he had wandered no greater distance
off. He showed his gratitude to his guides by presenting them with the two large holster pistols which
he brought with him from Oregon; and on the following morning they took their departure from the
camp.

CHAPTER XX.

The Author inclined to return to the coast—Sickness in the camp—Provisions
run low—What is to be done with the gold?—Proposal to convey it to the
coast—Short rations—Indians visit the camp—The invalids of the party—
The conveyance of the gold again discussed—Suspicions began to arise—
Captain Sutter's receipt missing—Bradley's explanation—Further discussions about the gold—The matter at last arranged—No chance of rain.

August 29th.—We have led a lazy life of it these last few
days. The excitement we have lately undergone has
unfitted us for regular labour ; and, besides, one has
had altogether a tolerably long spell of toil. Although,
ever since we have been fairly settled here—now about
a month—we have not worked more than from four
or five hours daily, and have taken it by turns to go
out on hunting expeditions : still I think most of us
have had enough of it; and were it not that the rainy
season will soon set in, when we shall be compelled
to give over work, I should, for my own part, feel
inclined to return to the coast forthwith. Sickness
has begun to show itself in our camp, and we have

H 3

three men now laid up: Bradshaw, whose wound, though healing, will still confine him for many days; Biggs, who has had a severe attack of fever, but is now recovering fast; and Dowling, who lies inside the shanty in an almost helpless state. My stock of drugs, too, is nearly exhausted. Thank God, my own health has altogether been most excellent. Although the vegetation dying off in the valleys at this time of the year gives rise to a sort of malaria, still, from the herbage not being of so rank a character about here as it is in the lower settlements, the effects are by no means so injurious; besides, the cool air from the mountains acts as a wholesome check.

Our provisions have run very low; nearly the whole of our flour is exhausted, and we are forced to live on the produce of our hunting expeditions. The little flour we have is set apart for the invalids of the party. Yesterday our hunters came in, after being absent all day, with only a black-tailed deer and a couple of hares: quails, however, are tolerably plentiful. Lacosse and the trapper have volunteered to set off to Sutter's, and bring us up a supply of breadstuffs sufficient to last us until the sickly season sets in. I believe it is arranged for them to start off to-morrow.

September 1*st.*—There have been several discussions as to the prudence of keeping the large quantity of gold we have already procured in camp, when we are liable to be surprised by the Indians, who for the sake of it would tomahawk and scalp us all round. It seems to have spread from tribe to tribe that the yellow earth which the pale faces are in search of will buy not only beads and buttons and red paint, but rifles, and charges of powder and ball, scarlet blankets, and the "strong water," which the Indian "loves, alas! not wisely but too well." Some are of the opinion that we ought to keep it by us, always leaving a proper guard on the look-out, until we finally abandon the digging, when we could return with it to the settlements in a body. Bradley and Don Luis are rather opposed to this plan, and volunteer to take the gold themselves to San Francisco or Monterey immediately, and deliver it into the custody of some merchant there on our joint account. I don't like this suggestion, for the amount is sufficiently large to tempt any one to make off with it; besides, it would be dangerous to send it without a strong guard. To-day we have put ourselves on short rations, as our stock of provisions is getting very low.

September 2*nd.*—The camp generally seem to be

in favour of Bradley's proposition. Some of the more
timid ones consider that we shall be in constant danger
for the next two months before the rainy season commences, when we must give over work. It is a great
pity that the gold was not sent down at the time
Lacosse and the trapper left.

Three Indians came into the camp last night, belonging, we believe, to some tribe no great distance
off. We gave them a good supper; and after it was
over we took care to make as much display as possible
of our fire-arms and bullet pouches, and to see that
our horses and mules were well tethered before we
turned in for the night. Story and M'Phail were the first
guard. The three Indians wrapped themselves up in
their blankets, and slept just outside the tent; and after
a good breakfast in the morning took their departure,
shaking hands with our party all round, and expressing
by other signs their satisfaction at the treatment they
had met with. Biggs is nearly recovered from his attack,
and will commence work again in a couple of days;
meanwhile, he is doing guard duty. Dowling and
Bradshaw are still both very ill.

September 3rd, Sunday.—Bradley repeated his
proposition to-day, that himself and Don Luis, accom-

panied by José, who was to take charge of a couple of
horses, with packs containing the bulk of the gold,
should start off the following morning. Story was of
opinion that they ought to be attended by a guard as
far as the Sacramento Valley ; but, to our surprise,
Bradley and Don Luis opposed this suggestion, on the
score that such a precaution was unnecessary.

Yesterday evening I took an opportunity of speak-
ing privately to Malcolm and M'Phail in reference
to Bradley's proposition, and also in reference to
his and Don Luis's peremptory dismissal of Story's
suggestion, without even allowing it to be discussed.
We then brought a circumstance to our recollection
which had never struck us before, namely, that neither
of us had ever seen Captain Sutter's receipt for the gold
Bradley had deposited in the Captain's charge, and we
determined to bring the matter up the first opportunity.
To-day, therefore, while we were at breakfast, Malcolm
asked Bradley if Captain Sutter had given a receipt for
the gold, when he answered " Yes, certainly ;" but, to
our surprise, stated that he had had the misfortune to
burn it. He went on to say, that while on his return
to Weber's Creek, during a halt he made, he had struck
a light for his cigar, 'and had incautiously used the

receipt for that purpose. He had mentioned the matter
to Don Luis, he said, the same day he returned.
Malcolm, M'Phail, and myself, looked at each other,
but we felt bound to believe Bradley's statement. We
arranged, however, during a stroll we made from the
camp, after breakfast was finished, not to agree to
Bradley's proposition in reference to the conveyance of
our present stock of gold, unless one of us three formed
one of the party accompanying it.

After dinner, I brought the subject forward by
observing, that if it was intended Bradley's plan
should be carried out, Malcolm would desire to form
one of the party ; and as an excuse for his going, I
stated that I wished him to get me a supply of drugs
at San Francisco, as the little stock I had brought
with me was quite exhausted ;— foolish - like, not
thinking at the time that Bradley and Don Luis could
have procured them quite as readily as Malcolm, and
that I was therefore giving no reason at all for his
accompanying them. Malcolm, however, came to my
relief, by stating he had business at San Francisco, as
he wished to see the captains of some of the vessels in
the harbour there that might be bound for the
Columbia River. Bradley gave Don Luis a side-look,

and said that no ships bound for the Columbia would be found at San Francisco at this time of the year. Biggs, however, who knew more about the shipping at that port than any of us, observed there would be; and rather a warm discussion ensued, which was interrupted by Story and M'Phail both saying to Bradley, that as Malcolm really wanted to go to San Francisco, they had better go in company. As there could be no possible objection to this course, it has been finally arranged for them to start off on the 5th (Tuesday). José was to be left behind.

The takings of the past week have been very good, considering that we have two of our party absent, and three laid up with illness. The sky has been a good deal overcast to-day ; but still, from what I learn, there is no chance of rain for another month.

CHAPTER XXI.

September 5th.— This morning, the party bound for
the coast started off as agreed on. We rose before
day-break, breakfasted, and got the horses in readiness just as the sun showed over the mountain. At
my suggestion, Malcolm had the strongest horse we
possessed allotted to him, as it had been arranged that
he should carry the bulk of the gold, and that Don
Luis and Bradley, who were to take as much as they
could carry in their saddle-bags, were to form the
guard. This plan was adopted in preference to having

a led horse, which it was thought would greatly impede their progress, and prevent the party from reaching the settlements on the Sacramento that night. Bradley and Don Luis each took with them eighteen pounds weight of gold : Malcolm, who was unencumbered by anything, and merely carried a brace of pistols in his belt, took very nearly seventy pounds. To relieve Malcolm's horse as much as possible, three of us, who were to act as an escort within a few miles of the Sacramento Valley, were each to carry fifteen pounds weight of the gold so far as we went. This escort was composed of Story, José, and myself.

We started off soon after sun-rise, amidst the faint cheers of our invalided companions, and, as it was necessary for the escorting party to return to the camp that night, it was agreed that we were to retrace our steps at noon or thereabouts. The commencement of our ride was through an open country, broken up by boulders of granite and clumps of dark grey sage trees, when, after ascending some low rocky hills, their summits crowned with a dense forest of gigantic pines, we entered a grassy valley, lined with groups of noble cedars, whose spreading branches offered a most inviting shade. Every now and then, we had to make our way down the sides of huge chasms which intercepted our progress, and then to toil slowly up the difficult ascent.

At noon we halted and took shelter from the sun in a little dell with a gushing spring bubbling up in the midst, and a patch of willows fringing the banks of the running stream. We scampered our horses down it, dismounted, and turning them loose to graze, seated ourselves at the base of a huge rock of granite. Our wallet of provisions was opened, and we soon made a hearty meal. Just as we had finished, some loose earth and a few small stones came tumbling down from above, knocking every now and then against the projecting ledges of rock in their descent. We immediately started up, thinking it might be some grizzly old bear anxious to make a meal of us, and Bradley and Malcolm scrambled up above to get a shot at him. But he had been too quick for them, for just as they reached the top, they heard the branches of the trees crackling in a tuft of underwood opposite, which lay between us and a deep water-course we had just crossed. As a fatiguing journey was before them, they did not think it worth while to give chase to the brute, and were on the point of descending again into the little hollow where they had left us, when the print of a man's foot caught Bradley's eye in the soft sandy earth. Several others were noticed close by, none of which, Bradley protested, had been made by our party, and certainly not by a bear, but by some sculking Indians, who had been very likely hovering about us. They hastened to communicate this intelligence to us, and it was decided that as the party bound for the coast were now within some few hours' ride of the upper settlements on the Sacramento, no Indians would be daring enough to attack them, and it would hardly be worth while for us to accompany them further. We, however, insisted upon riding a few miles more on the road, which having done, we took leave of them with many wishes for their safe and speedy return, and turned our horse's heads round in the direction of the camp.

Feeling rather fidgetty at the incident of the morning, we passed the spot where it had taken place, keeping an anxious look-out in every direction, and after a hard ride of several hours, reached the camp shortly after sundown, glad that we had escaped any disaster. We had a merry evening of it; a double allowance of whisky was served out, and we drank our friends' safe arrival and return.

I now sit down for the first time, after a lapse of several weeks, to resume the continuation of my narrative. Late in the evening of the 5th, while my companions were chatting over the fire, and I was engaged in writing, we were interrupted on a sudden by a loud whistle, the note of which I thought I could not be mistaken in. "Sure that's Bradley," exclaimed I ; the others thought not, and catching up their rifles, examined the flints. The whistle, when again repeated, convinced every one, however, that my first surmise had been correct. In another minute Bradley galloped up to us, and Don Luis soon followed after ; but, to our astonishment, Malcolm was not of the party. "My friends," exclaimed Bradley, "a sad disaster; the best part of the gold is gone—lost beyond a doubt." "Lost!" said I, expecting some treachery on the part of Bradley and Don Luis ; "How? I don't believe it; I never will believe it." Bradley gave me an angry look, but said nothing.

"Where's Malcolm?" exclaimed I. "Dead by this time, I am afraid," replied Bradley. "Good God!" I exclaimed aloud, and involuntarily muttered to myself, "Then you have murdered him." I noticed Bradley examined the countenances of the whole party by turns, and as my eye followed his, I saw that every one looked sullen and angry. He, too, evidently saw this, and said nothing more the whole evening. Don Luis, however, volunteered the following explanation of the mystery.

He informed us that, after we had parted from them, they put their horses into a quick trot, to escape as soon as possible into a more agreeable-looking sort of country. They suspected some vagabond Indians were hovering about, and as the ground they were travelling over afforded too many opportunities of concealment to gentry of their character, they were anxious to reach a more open district. Their road lay, for several miles, over a succession of small hills, intersected by valleys covered with stunted oak trees, and with here and there a solitary pine. Just at a point, when they were winding round a ridge of hills, which they imagined separated them from the Sacramento Valley, having a small skirting of timber on their left hand, he, Don Luis, being slightly in advance of Bradley and Malcolm, happened to turn his head round, when he saw a horseman stealthily emerging from the thicket, at a point a short distance in their rear. In a very few moments another horseman joined the first, and before

Don Luis could give an alarm, the second rider,
who, it seems, was an Indian, had risen in his saddle
and had flung out his lasso, which, whizzing through
the air true to its aim, descended over Malcolm's head
and shoulders. Don Luis, who saw all this, immediately
jumped from his horse, and, placing his finger on the
trigger of his rifle, fired just as the Indian was galloping
away. The ball entered his horse's head, when the
beast was brought to a stand, and, in a second of time,
rolled over with its rider beneath it, just as the noose
had tightened, and Malcolm was being drawn off his
horse to the ground. Bradley, who only knew of the
danger they were in by hearing the lasso whirl through
the air, immediately dismounted, and, like Don Luis,
sheltered himself behind his horse, while he took aim
and fired. His never-failing rifle brought down one of
their enemies, a swarthy-looking man in the usual
Mexican sombrero, off his horse to the ground. In the
twinkling of an eye they led their horses behind some
boulders of granite which afforded them cover, and
from behind which they saw four men come charging
down upon them. But Bradley and Don Luis, skilled
in this kind of warfare, had already stooped down and
reloaded. Don Luis was the first to let fly at the

advancing party, but without success. His shot was answered by a discharge of rifles from the enemy, which whistled over his and Bradley's heads. Crack went Bradley's rifle again—"And you would have thought," said Don Luis to us, " that the ball had split into four pieces, and had given each man a tender touch, for they wheeled round their horses in an instant, and galloped off, driving Malcolm's horse before them, which we never saw again."

Don Luis then went on to say, that as soon as they saw the coast was clear, they left their cover and sought out Malcolm, who was lying on the ground with the lasso tightly pinioning his arms, and to all appearance dead. On a closer examination, however, they found that he still breathed, and also that he had been severely trampled on by some of the horses of the robbers in their retreat. Bradley pulled out his bowie-knife and cut the lasso in a few moments, when they tried to raise him up, but found that the injuries he had sustained prevented him from standing. He was, in fact, quite insensible. At that moment they were alarmed by the sound of voices, and looking round they saw a party of horsemen riding up at full speed from the direction of the Sacramento.

They gave themselves up for lost, but, to their delight, the new-comers proved to be a party of miners, who hearing so many rifle-reports in such rapid succession, had immediately hastened to the spot. Don Luis supposed that the robbers had seen their approach, and that this, and not the bullet from Bradley's rifle, had been the cause of the scoundrels' precipitate retreat. They found the Indian's horse, to the saddle of which the lasso was attached, quite dead. The Indian himself had managed to crawl off, though doubtless much hurt, as Don Luis saw the horse roll right over him. The body of the robber shot by Bradley was found; life was quite extinct, the ball having passed through his chest in a transverse direction, evidently penetrating the heart. He was recognised by some of the miners—natives of the country —as one of the disbanded soldiers of the late Californian army, by name Tomas Maria Carillo; a man of the very worst character, who had connected himself with a small band of depredators, whose occupation was to lay in wait at convenient spots along the roads in the neighbourhood of the sea-coast, and from thence to pounce upon and plunder any unfortunate merchant or ranchero that might be passing unprotected that way. The gang had now evidently abandoned the coast to try their fortune in the neighbourhood of the mines, and, judging from the accounts which one of the miners gave of the number of robberies that had recently taken place about there, their mission had been eminently successful.

" Our first care," continued Don Luis, " was to see to poor Malcolm, and our next object was to go in pursuit of the ruffians. On intimating as much to our new friends, to our surprise they declined to render us any assistance. Their curiosity, which it seems was the only motive that brought them towards us, had been satisfied, and I felt disgusted at the brutality of their conduct when they coolly turned their horses' heads round, and left us alone with our dying friend, not deigning further to notice our appeals to them for assistance. No, they must set to work again, digging and washing, and we might thank ourselves that their coming up had saved *our* lives; this was the burthen of their reply. In their eager pursuit of gold, they had not a moment to spare for the commonest offices of Christian charity. At length," said Don Luis, " in answer to my passionate expostulations, backed by the offer of any reward they might demand—which offer

I

alone gave force to my words—two of them consented
to return in about an hour with a litter to convey
Malcolm to their camp.

" The litter they brought was formed of branches of
trees tied together,, and covered thickly over with
blankets. On this Malcolm was slowly borne down
the hill-side, until a rude shanty was reached. He
was carried inside, and we were fortunate enough to
meet with a kind Californian woman, who promised to
attend on him while we returned here for your assistance."

In reply to my inquiries, Don Luis said that he
thought there were no bones broken, but poor Malcolm was dreadfully bruised, and his flesh in parts
much lacerated. He feared, however, that he had
experienced some severe internal injuries. At it was
utterly impossible for me to have found my way to
him that night, I determined to take a short nap and
hurry to him the following morning.

During Don Luis's recital I did not for one
moment think of the gold which we had lost; all my
sympathies were with my poor friend. But, at the conclusion of Don Luis's narrative, I saw that but few of
my associates participated in my grief. Don Luis was

immediately assailed with inquiries rudely addressed to him in reference to the missing gold. In reply, he stated that we all knew that Malcolm carried in his saddle-bags the great bulk of the gold they were conveying to San Francisco ; and that, of course, when the robbers drove off the horse, the gold went with it. " It is the doctor you have to thank for that," growled out Bradley ; and though I could not see the matter in this light, still I could not help thinking of my own distrustful disposition, which, in reality, had been the cause of making Malcolm a party to the conveyance of the treasure : this, in fact, had in all probability sacrificed my friend's life. I thought of his poor wife and children in Oregon, who would be waiting in vain for his return, which he, poor fellow, had delayed so long, in the hope of going back to them laden with wealth. Thoughout the whole of the night most of the party remained gathered around the camp-fire — now in sullen silence, and now expressing their bitter dissatisfaction at the arrangements which had led to the day's misfortune. And when the first faint light of daybreak showed over the tall peaks of the snowy mountains, it discovered us looking haggard and dejected, alike wearied and disgusted with everything around.

CHAPTER XXII.

WE made a hasty meal from our scanty stock of provisions on the morning of the 6th, and directly it was over—just as I was about saddling my horse, to start off to visit poor Malcolm—Don Luis informed me that our companions seemed all to be of opinion that it would be best to share the stock of gold still remaining at once, when those that preferred it could make their way to the settlements, and the others could continue working, if they pleased, on their own account. I had no objection to offer to this proposition, and the gold was all collected together and weighed. Bradley undertook the charge of Lacosse's share, and I was requested to convey Malcolm's to him. Altogether we scraped up nearly forty-two pounds weight; for, besides the gold which Don Luis and Bradley had in their saddle-bags, there were a few pounds more belonging to the general stock. This had to be divided equally, for the gold we had brought from Weber's Creek had been confided to Malcolm's charge in a separate bag. It gave exactly four pounds two ounces a man—value seven hundred dollars. This, with six hundred and fifty dollars, my share of the gold deposited with Captain Sutter, and the dust, scales, and lumps, arising from my share of the sale of the cradles, and the produce at the Mormon diggings, before Lacosse and Biggs joined us, would amount, in the whole, to over fifteen hundred dollars.

The greater part of the morning was taken up with squabbles respecting the weighing of the gold. I took no part in it, and was content to receive just what was allotted to me. I called M'Phail aside, and asked him what it was he intended doing. He replied, that if any of the others would join him, he would start in pursuit of the men who had plundered us. He was sorry the old trapper was not here, as, with his assistance, he felt certain the scoundrels might be ferreted out. Feeling that the journey to poor

Malcolm was too dangerous a one to be attempted alone, I was compelled to wait until I could prevail on some of the party to join me. Don Luis, José, Bradley, M'Phail, and myself, at length arranged to start off. Biggs, who was now quite well, preferred waiting behind a few days longer. Neither Bradshaw nor Dowling were sufficiently recovered to travel. Story determined to wait until they were well enough to accompany him. I hardly liked the notion of leaving these four men behind—only two, or at most three, of them able to protect themselves in the event of their being attacked; still they did not seem to fear the danger: though, even if they had, most of us had grown so selfish and unaccommodating, that I don't think they would have met with much sympathy.

It was an hour beyond noon when we were in readiness to start. We took two of the baggage-horses with us, to carry the tent-poles and covering, and a few utensils. Our personal baggage was packed on the horses we rode. Bradley and Don Luis rode in advance, José followed with the baggage-horses, and M'Phail and myself brought up the rear. We had not proceeded more than four miles on the

trail when we saw a couple of horsemen some distance
ahead, advancing towards us.   As soon as we were
within a couple of hundred yards of each other, we
at once recognised them to be Lacosse and the old
trapper.   Urging our horses into a smart trot, we
soon arrived alongside of them; and, on inquiring
what it was that had caused them to remain so
long at Sutter's, and also how it was that they had
neither the baggage horses nor, apparently, any provisions with them, Lacosse gave us this explanation.

He stated that after leaving the camp, they struck
the Sacramento River that night, and succeeded in
reaching the upper settlements towards evening on the
following day.   The next morning they pursued their
journey and arrived at Sutter's Fort about sundown :
they encamped near here for the night.   Flour was as
much as eighty-five dollars a barrel, and everything in
the way of provisions was in the same proportion. They
purchased a stock of flour, and packing their horses,
moved off the same day.   In the evening they encamped
some fifteen miles up the Sacramento, near the mouth
of the Feather River, and within a hundred yards of the
spot where the Indian village existed which Captain
Sutter had destroyed ; the whole circumstances con

nected with which we had already heard from the old trapper. They resumed the journey early on the following morning, and by the evening had made about twenty-five miles, when they rested for the night near one of the little camps of miners, which they found scattered about the valley every few miles along the route. The next day they pushed forward, and found these encampments much less numerous—only one or two were passed throughout the entire day. Just after sundown, however, they saw by the fires up the hills quite a little colony of gold-washers, which they moved towards; and, after purchasing some provisions at a store recently opened there, for which they paid a most exorbitant price, they securely tethered their horses to stakes they had driven in the ground, and encamped for the night. They did not think it necessary to keep watch, but when they awoke in the morning they found the baggage-horses had been driven off, and their packs stolen. The horses they had been riding on were just as they had left them over night. The trail-marks around the camp were too numerous to make anything out of them.

On making inquiries at several of the tents, they were treated in a very cavalier sort of manner. No one, of course, knew anything about their horses and packs, and one big bony American even threatened to put a rifle-ball into them unless they left his shanty. This was rather too much for them to swallow quietly, so they rated the fellow in round terms; but he very coolly reached his rifle down from a shelf above him, and told them that he would give them time to consider whether they would move off or not while he examined his flint, and if they were not gone by that time, he would make a hole in each of their skulls, one after the other. Finding that he was coolly preparing to carry out his threat, they made their exit, and found some ten or twelve people gathered together outside. From one of them Lacosse learnt that this man had shot two people since he had fixed himself at this spot, and that he was a terror to most of the miners in the camp. It appears to have been no uncommon thing among them for a man to settle a quarrel by severely disabling his adversary. There were several people at work down by the river, with their arms in slings, who had received serious injuries in quarrels with some of their fellows.

They thought it best to escape from such a state of things with as little delay as possible, and immediately mounted their horses and pursued their journey. That night they took good care to encamp far enough off from any of the gold-finding fraternity.

It was now our turn to explain to Lacosse the reason of our return to the settlements, and the unfortunate circumstances that had led to it. He was disappointed enough at the intelligence. He said that he should go on to the fort and collect his baggage together, and would, if possible, join Don Luis, Bradley, and M'Phail at Sutter's, and see whether any plan could be arranged on for recovering our stolen treasure. The trapper was to accompany him, and it was agreed that either Bradley or M'Phail should await their arrival at Sutter's Fort.

We resumed our journey, and at sundown fixed our tent at the bottom of a steep hollow, and supped off the moderate rations we had brought with us from the camp. The night was quite frosty, and when I awoke in the morning, my limbs were numbed with cold. We prepared our coffee, and partook of our slight breakfast, then saddling the horses, resumed our march. It was late in the evening when we reached the rude shanty to which poor Malcolm had been conveyed a couple of days since. It was an

anxious moment to me; but I was gratified to find
that he had so far recovered from the injuries he had
sustained as to be able to sit up and to take some little
nourishment. He told me that beyond the severe
bruises with which his body was covered, and a wound in
the fleshy part of his leg, he did not think he was
otherwise injured. Throughout the whole of yesterday
he had experienced the most violent pains in his
head; but a comfortable sleep into which he had
fallen last night had, to all appearances, entirely de
prived him of them. He was troubled though, he
told me, with a sickening sensation, which made him
loathe anything in the shape of food. I at once
prescribed such remedies as I thought necessary to
be applied immediately, and left him in charge of his
kind nurse until the morning.

I was at his bedside shortly after the sun rose, and
watched by him until he awoke. Another good night's
rest had greatly benefited him. During the day,
recurring to his misfortune, he told me that when the
lasso first fell over his shoulders, he fancied for the
moment that he was in the gripe of some wild beast,
but immediately he felt himself drawn from his
horse, the truth became apparent to him. He was

stunned by the fall, and lay insensible on the ground, quite unconscious that the horse of one of the robbers had trampled upon him, as had evidently been the case.

Don Luis, Bradley, M'Phail, and José left us about noon on their way to Sutter's Fort. I promised to rejoin them in a few days, if Malcolm so far recovered as no longer to be in need of my services. I was in great hopes of such a result, as he showed evident signs of improvement since I saw him the previous day.

CHAPTER XXIII.

The gold district—Sickness and selfishness—The dead become the prey of the
wolf—Malcolm's gradual recovery—The kindness of his nurse—A malaria
—Life and property alike insecure—The wealthy gold-finder laid in wait
for—Bodies in the river—Gold for a pillow—Robberies—Rags—Brandy
at a dollar a dram—The big bony American again—Sutter's Fort—Intelligence of Lacosse—Intelligence of the robbers—Sweeting's Hotel again—
A meeting—" El Capitan "—Desertions from the ships—Andreas offer to a
captain—The first Alcalde gone to the mines—The second Alcalde follows
his superior—Start for Monterey in pursuit of Andreas—Board the vessels
in port—A deserter arrested—Leave Monterey—Cross the coast range—
Meet with civilized Indians—Intelligence of the robbers—Indian horse-
stealers—Continue the pursuit—Abandon it and return to Monterey.

I STAYED with Malcolm throughout the next few
days, and spent a good part of my time out of doors
among the gold-washers, but still I felt no inclination
to take part in their labours. Fever was very prevalent, and I found that more than two-thirds of the
people at this settlement were unable to move out of
their tents. The other third were too selfish to render
them any assistance. The rainy season was close at
hand, when they would have to give over work, but
meanwhile they sought after the gold as though all their
hopes of salvation rested on their success. I was told
that deaths were continually taking place, and that

the living comrades of those whose eyes were closed in that last sleep when " the wicked cease from troubling and the weary are at rest," denied the poor corpses of their former friends a few feet of earth for a grave, and left the bodies exposed for the wolf to prey upon.

In a couple of days Malcolm was sufficiently recovered no longer to require my assistance. At his instigation, I took my departure towards Sutter's Fort, where M'Phail or Lacosse might perhaps still be waiting for me. I felt that he was in good hands, and that his kind Californian nurse and her husband would do all that they could for him. Their kind treatment of my poor friend offered a striking contrast to the callous selfishness around.

I journeyed by slow marches along the banks of the Sacramento, passing several colonies of gold-finders on my way. At noon I halted at one of these, and loitered some little time round about the camp. The rapidly-decaying vegetation—here unusually rank —was producing a malaria, and sickness was doing its ravages; but still the poor infatuated people, or rather such of them as were not prevented by positive inability, worked on until they sunk under the toil.

Every one seemed determined to labour as hard as possible for the few weeks left before the rainy season set in, and the result was, that many of them met their deaths.   There were others, though, who sought to enrich themselves with the shining gold by a quicker and, perhaps, less dangerous process than all this weary toil.

According to the accounts I heard, life and property were alike insecure.   The report ran, that as soon as it became known that a man had amassed a large amount of gold, he was watched and followed about till an opportunity presented itself of quietly putting him out of the way.   There had been but few known deaths, but the number of persons who had been missed, and whose own friends even had not thought it worth while to go in search of them, was very large.   In every case the man's stock of gold was not to be found in his tent; still there was nothing surprising in this, as every one made a point of carrying his gold about him, no matter how heavy it might happen to be.   One or two dead bodies had been found floating in the river, which circumstance was looked upon as indicative of foul play having taken place, as it was considered that the poorest of the gold-finders carried fully a sufficient weight of gold about them to cause their bodies to sink to the bottom of the stream. Open attempts at robbery were rare; it was in the stealthy night time that thieves prowled about, and, entering the little tents, occupied by not more than perhaps a couple of miners, neither of whom, in all probability, felt inclined to keep a weary watch over their golden treasure, carried off as much of it as they could lay their hands on. By way of precaution, however, almost every one slept with their bag of gold underneath their pillow, having a rifle or revolver within their reach.

That same night I reached the camp of gold-washers, where Lacosse and the trapper had had their horses and packs of provisions stolen from them. The robbery, I believe, was committed by men almost on the verge of want, who thought it a more convenient way of possessing themselves of a stock of provisions than performing a journey to the lower settlements for that purpose would have been, and a cheaper way than purchasing them here, where they run scarce, and where the price of them is exorbitantly high. Other things are in proportion. Clothing of any description is hardly to be had at any price, and

the majority of the miners go about in rags. Collected
round a rude shanty, where brandy was being dis-
pensed at a dollar a dram! I saw a group of ragged
gold-diggers, the greater part of them suffering from
fever, paying this exorbitant price for glass after glass
of the fiery spirit ; every drop of which they consumed
was only aggravating their illness, and, in all probability, bringing them one step nearer to their grave.

The big bony American, who treated Lacosse and
the trapper in such a peremptory manner, and who
seemed to be the terror of these diggings, was pointed
out to me. I learnt, however, that he had accumulated
a very large amount of gold, over sixteen thousand
dollars' worth, it was said ; and his suspicions that
parties were lying in wait to plunder him of it, was
the cause of his acting as he had done. He thought
they only came to his shanty with an excuse, for the
purpose of observing its weak points, and that no
doubt they had a scheme in their heads for robbing
him, either at night time, or while he was absent
digging and washing during the day. The men he
had shot, it seems, were common thieves — one, a
deserter from the garrison at Monterey, and the other
belonging to a similar band of robbers to that by

which our party had been attacked, and our gold carried off.

I reached Sutter's Fort the next day, and found it like the most crowded localities of some of our great cities, with the exception that the bulk of the people we met with belonged to a totally different race. I saw Captain Sutter for a few moments, when he informed me that Mr. Bradley and his party had left a couple of days ago; and that a gentleman, accompanied by a man named Joe White, who, as the Captain said, used to trap for him before the gold fever came up, had been making inquiries at the Fort respecting Mr. Bradley that very day. I at once saw that this could be no other than Lacosse, and set off to see if I could meet with him. After some search, I was fortunate enough to discover him at the newly opened hotel here, where he had intended stopping for the night. I remained with him and shared his room—a little box not more than ten feet by twelve, or thereabouts; but we considered ourselves fortunate in having obtained even that, the place being tremendously crowded.

I heard from Lacosse that Captain Sutter had informed him that the leader of the band of desperadoes who had plundered us, had been seen down at the Fort with some of his companions not more than ten days ago. He was quite sure he was right in the man ; for Tomas Maria, who had been shot, belonged to his gang, and was, in fact, his chief lieutenant. The name of El Capitan was Andreas Armjo ; and Captain Sutter said he recommended Bradley to make his way to San Francisco, where, in all probability, he would meet with him, as when he left the Fort he had taken the road towards the coast.

The nevt day we started off towards San Francisco, and, from inquiries made on the road, found that we were on the correct track—Bradley, Don Luis, M'Phail, and José, having passed through a day or two previous. We arrived at the end of our journey without meeting with any adventures worth noting, and at once made our way to Sweeting's hotel, glad to find it one of the few houses in this town that were not shut up. Here we met with our friends, who had been there now nearly two days, and were then on the point of starting off in pursuit of Andreas and his comrades. We learned from them, that directly they heard the important information which Captain Sutter had communicated to them, they started of in pursuit, but not with any expectation of coming up with the gentlemen they were in search of before arriving at San Francisco. They had constant tidings of them all along the route, as El Capitan was too well known to many a poor ranchero whom he had plundered of the dollars produced by the sale of his hides, while on his journey home from the sea-coast.

When they arrived at San Francisco, they made inquiries whether any ships had recently left the harbour, and were glad to find that there was not a merchant vessel in port with enough hands on board to weigh the anchor. Every ship had been more or less deserted by its crews, who had hastened off for a few weeks' labour at the gold diggings. They found, however, that Andreas Armjo and his men had been making inquiries on board of several of the vessels to ascertain when any of them left port. On finding none were sufficiently manned to do so, they offered the captain of one schooner a thousand dollars to land them at any port in Mexico he pleased, and said they would themselves help to work the ship. The captain, however, declined the offer.

After receiving this intelligence, they went to the house of the first alcalde, to consult with him on

what steps should be taken to arrest the robbers, who
were then doubtless at some place near the coast.
They found, however, that he had gone to the mines
with the rest of the people, and they made their way to
the residence of the second alcalde, in the hope of being
more fortunate ; but he too had gone to the mines with
his superior. Further inquiries satisfied them that
there was not an officer of justice left in the town of
San Francisco, and they had therefore determined to
make their way forthwith to Monterey, as, in all probability, the gang would proceed there in the hope of
meeting with a ship.

Lacosse and myself determined to accompany them,
and the old trapper volunteered his services, which
were accepted.   We obtained fresh horses from Sweeting, and set off in gallant style, determined to shorten
the distance by hard riding. It was early on Wednesday
morning when we arrived at Monterey ; and M'Phail
and Bradley proceeded to board all the ships in the
bay, while Don Luis, Lacosse, and myself made
inquiries about the town.   We soon learnt that Andreas Amjo and his party had been paying it a visit ;
and, moreover, one of the gang, who thought he had
disguised himself so as not to be recognised, had been

seized as a deserter from the garrison here. The others were not interfered with, as there was no specific charge out against them. Our robbery had, of course, not been heard of here. Don Luis and myself, after having dispatched Lacosse to communicate this intelligence to Bradley and M'Phail, sought an interview with Colonel Mason, and, on informing him of the robbery and the circumstances attending it, received from him an order to see the soldier who was then under arrest. By promises of not proceeding against him, for any share he might have had in the robbery, we induced him to confess the whole circumstances connected with it, and also to inform us of the route intended to be taken by El Capitan and the two others of the gang. This, it seems, was along the great Spanish Trail to Santa Fé.

On rejoining our companions, we decided to continue here the remainder of the day, and to start off the next morning in pursuit. We informed Colonel Mason of the circumstance, and he stated that he would have furnished us with a guard to accompany us, if he did not feel certain that the men would desert to the mines directly they got outside the town.

At four o'clock the next morning we commenced the journey, each of us taking a stock of provisions sufficient to last for a fortnight ; although we hoped, and fully expected, that we should be back to Monterey several days before that time had expired. It was purely a question of hard riding. Andreas and his party had started, as far as we could learn, three days in advance of us, and no doubt knew the track better than the old trapper who had undertaken to accompany us as guide. He had never penetrated further than the foot of the Sierra, so that if we were compelled to cross the mountains we should have to seek for some Indians to guide us on our course. By pressing our horses hard we succeeded in crossing the hills of the coast range that night, and encamped some slight way down the descent, in as sheltered a spot as we could manage to select. The night was quite frosty, but we made up a blazing fire, and, well wrapped up in our serapes, slept till morning, without feeling much inconvenience from the cold. Next day we struck the river of the lakes, and found it thickly hemmed in with timber along its whole course. We soon found a fording place, and encamped at night a few miles from the east bank. The following morning we fell in with some civilized Indians, who informed us, in answer to our inquiries, that a party of three whites passed along the trail the evening before last, and that they would have encamped at no great distance from this spot.

These Indians, Don Luis informed me, had all of them been attached to the Californian Missions; but, since the downfall of these establishments, they had moved across the coast range, and had located themselves in the neighbourhood of the Tule Lakes, subsisting chiefly on horseflesh. To gratify their appetites, however, instead of giving chase to the number of wild horses—here called mustangs—that are scattered over the extensive prairies in the neighbourhood of the lakes, they adopt a much lazier method of supplying their larder. This is, to make predatory excursions across the mountains, and to drive off a large herd of tame horses, belonging to some poor ranchero, at a time; these they slaughter, and subsist on as long as the flesh lasts, when they set out again on a similar expedition. Sometimes they are pursued, and, if overtaken, butchered forthwith; but, in general, they manage to escape some little distance into the interior, where they are safe not to be followed.

We put spurs into our horses, and soon cleared the marshy ground intervening between us and the Fork, which we forded, and rode for several miles through a country thickly covered over with oak trees, and intersected by numerous small rivulets. Large herds of elk were frequently started, and during the whole day their shrill whistle was continually being heard.

We encamped to-night without having heard anything more of Andreas Armjo and his companions. Several parties of Indians we met a few hours before sundown stated that they had not seen any white men along the trail. I felt disposed, as far as I was myself concerned, to give over the pursuit, as my horse was already worn out by the journey; but my companions would not listen to it, and determined, at any rate, to see what would result from following it up briskly during the next day. We had all noticed that there were no new signs of horses that had been shod passing along the trail, but Bradley was of opinion that the party would be mounted on unshod beasts, as very few of the native Californians had their horses shod, unless they were going a journey across a rough broken country.

Next day we fell in with several more parties of

Indians, from whom we learnt that the men we were
in pursuit of were full two days' journey before us.
One party, who had seen them encamped the preceding evening more than forty miles a-head, told us
that they had inquired of them where the trail turned
off to Los Angelos. As this town was at least five or
six days' journey distant, and as the Sierra had to be
crossed to reach it, we concluded among ourselves
that it would be best for us to return to Monterey
forthwith. This decision was readily come to, as there
was now no hope of overtaking the party, and every
step we proceeded we were getting into a more hostile
country. In all probability, if we had pursued them
to Los Angelos, we should have discovered that they
had struck off on to the great Spanish Trail, as was
their original intention, or else have found that they
had been to Los Angelos, and had taken their departure for some other place on the coast.

We therefore turned our horses' heads, and retraced
our steps towards the coast in no merry mood. We
rode along, in fact, in sullen silence, only broken to
mutter out our expressions of disappointment at the
escape of those who had robbed us of the fruits of
so many months of toil, exposure, and hardship.

We encountered nothing very remarkable during our three day's journey to Monterey. There were the same prairies to cross, the same thickets to penetrate, and the same streams to ford. Herds of elk and mustangs were continually seen upon the heights, and every now and then we met with some small parties of Indians, many of the chiefs dressed in the Spanish fashion. We were too well armed, and too many in number, for any of them to venture to attack us, had they been so inclined; but generally their intentions seemed to be perfectly pacific.

CHAPTER XXIV.

The Author and his friends part company—Their regrets at the separation—
Friendship in the wilderness—Friendship at a supper—The Author finds
himself alone—Monterey deserted.—High wages—Officers' servants not to
be obtained—A few arrivals from the mines—Stores shut, houses blocked
up, and ships left defenceless.

WE had previously determined, on arriving at the
sea-coast, to part company. There was now no object
for keeping together in a party, and our future plans
were, of course, very undecided. It was, therefore,
clearly advisable that we should, at least for the present, separate. This resolution was not come to without
something like a pang—a pang which I sincerely felt,
and which I believe was more or less experienced by
us all. We had lived for four months in constant
companionship—we had undergone hardships and
dangers together, and a friendship, more vivid than
can well be imagined in civilized lands to have been
the growth of so short a period, had sprung up betwixt
us. There had been a few petty bickerings between
as, and some unjust suspicions on my part in respect to
Bradley; but these were all forgotten. Common sense,

however, dictated the dissolution of our party. When we reached Monterey, we went to an inferior sort of hotel, but the best open ; and the following day we arranged the division of the proceeds arising from the sale of the gold that Bradley had left with Captain Sutter for consignment here. The same night we had a supper, at which a melancholy species of joviality was in the ascendant, and the next day shook hands and parted. Don Luis went back to his own pleasant home, and Bradley started for San Francisco. As for the others, I hardly know what were their destinations. All I know is, that on waking the next morning, I found that I was alone.

After breakfast I walked about the town. Like San Francisco, Monterey has been nearly deserted. Everybody has gone to the diggings, leaving business, ships, and stores, to take care of themselves. The persons who remain are either persons carrying on profitable branches of commerce, the very existence of which requires the presence of principals upon the spot, and their clerks and servants, who have been tempted by high wages to stay. To give an idea of the rate of remuneration paid, I may mention that salesmen and shopmen have been receiving at the rate of from two thousand three hundred to two thousand seven hundred dollars, with their board, per annum. Mere boys get extravagant salaries in the absence of their seniors; and the lowest and most menial offices are paid for at a rate which only such a wonderful influx of gold would render credible.

But, even with the inducement of this high pay, it was found exceedingly difficult to retain the services of persons engaged in commercial and domestic capacities. I learned from Colonel Mason that the officers in garrison at Monterey had not been able for two months to command the assistance of a servant. Indeed, they had been actually obliged either to cook their own dinners, or to go without. Every one had taken his turn in the culinary department, and even Colonel Mason had not been exempted.

The prevalence of sickness at the mines has sent a few people back here; but, with the commencement of the rainy season, I anticipate that there will be plenty of labour in the market, and that its value will become correspondingly depreciated. In the meantime, the general aspect of the town is forlorn and deserted; stores are shut, houses blocked up, and in the harbour ships ride solitary and defenceless.

CHAPTER XXV.

Letter from the Author to his Brother in England.

MONTEREY, *October 11th*, 1848.

DEAR GEORGE,—I take advantage of the departure of a courier sent by Colonel Mason, the United States Governor of California, to Washington, with dispatches, to let you know what I have been about during the five months which have elapsed since I last wrote you. Long before you receive this you will have heard in England of the extraordinary occurrences which have taken place out here. My last letter, which I hope you received, told you of the failure of the emigration scheme to Oregon, and of my intention of leaving that barren, desert-like place, the first possible opportunity. A friend of mine, of whom I have before spoken to you, namely, Mr. Malcolm, a Scotchman, and a thorough practical agriculturist, was anxious to shift his quarters to California, the soil of which country was represented by every one who had visited it as of extra-ordinary fertility. We had heard of the war that was

going on between the United States and Mexico
having extended itself to that country, and Mr.
Malcolm prevailed on me to accompany him to San
Francisco, where he thought I might manage to obtain
an appointment in the United States army. We made
the voyage together, and the accompanying diary—of
which more by-and-bye—commences with an account
of our first setting out.

But to return to California. I assure you it is
hardly possible for any accounts of the gold mines, and
of what I may call gold gravel and sand, to be
exaggerated. The El Dorado of the early voyagers to
America has really been discovered; and what its
consequences may be, not only upon this continent,
but upon the world, wiser heads—heads more versed
than mine is in monetary science—must tell. There
is much speculation here as to the effects which the
late wonderful discovery will produce in the States
and the old country. Of course we expect to be
inundated with emigrants, coming, I suppose, from
every part of the world, and truly, for all I can tell, there
will be gold enough for all.

And now, the first question you will ask me is,
whether I have made my fortune ? I reply, my old

bad luck has not forsaken me. I always seem to come in for monkey's allowance—more kicks than halfpence. Three months ago I thought my fortune was made, and that I might come home a South American nabob. Nothing of the kind. Here I was, almost on the spot, when the first news of the gold was received. I have worked hard, and undergone some hardships, and, thanks to the now almost lawless state of this country, I have been deprived of the great mass of my savings, and must, when the dry season comes round again, set to work almost anew. I have but fourteen hundred dollars' worth of the precious metal remaining, and, with the rate of prices which now universally prevails here, that will not keep me much over a couple of months. My own case, though, is that of many others. As the number of diggers and miners augmented, robberies and violence became frequent. At first, when we arrived at the Mormon diggings, for example, everything was tranquil. Every man worked for himself, without disturbing his neighbour. Now the scene is widely changed indeed. When I was last there, as you will see by my diary, things were bad enough ; but now, according to the reports we hear, no man, known to be in possession of much gold, dare say, as he lays down his head at night, that he will ever rise from his pillow. The fact is, that there is no executive government of any strength here to put an end to this state of things. The country is almost a wilderness, whereof Indians are the principal inhabitants. The small force Colonel Mason has here has been thinned very materially by desertions, and the fidelity of those that remain is, according to the opinion of their commanding officer, not to be over much depended on.

Of course, as you may expect, I am naturally much cast down at the turn which matters have taken—I mean as regards my own misfortune. It is heartbreaking to be robbed by a set of villains of what you have worked so hard for, and have undergone so much to obtain. I am in hopes, however, that my next gold campaign may be a more successful one. I dare say there have been plenty of accounts of the doings in California in the newspapers. As, however, not only you, but Anna and Charley, and my kind friends Mr. and Mrs. ———— and Miss ————, and many others, will, I am sure, be glad to know something about my own personal adventures, I send you a rough diary of

what I have seen and done. I hardly know whether
you will be able to make the whole of it out, for I
have interlined it in many parts, and my writing never
was of the most legible character. You know I have
always been in the habit, ever since I first went abroad,
of jotting down some record of my movements, scanty
enough, but still forming a memorial which it is pleasant to look back upon. As, however, the gold affair
is not only a great feature in a man's life, but in the
history of our times, I made pretty full jottings of my
adventures every few days ; and since I returned here,
I have spent several days in expanding them, and add-
ing to them a few extra particulars which I thought
would be of interest. I don't know whether you will
care to wade through such a bundle of information
The MS. when I got it all together quite frightened me,
and I hardly liked to ask Colonel Mason to transmit
such a bulky parcel for me ; but you know our couriers
over here travel with quite a cavalcade of horses, and
a few pounds more would not be thought much of.
However, as it may prove interesting to yourself—
S——— I know will read it through with pleasure
and delight in it—I dispatch it for you to do as you
like with. It will be forwarded to a young friend of

mine in New York, Mr. Thorne, to whom I have
written, requesting him to transmit the package to
England by one of the monthly steamers.   This will
save you a heavy charge for postage, which, I dare say,
you would not thank me for.

You can't conceive, my dear brother, how often I
have wished you were out here with me.   Your engi-
neering talents would have been invaluable in invent-
ing some method of procuring the gold dust, or rather
of separating it from the soil, which would have been
much more effectual than the rude way in which we
went to work.   At the same time, I am now thankful
you are at home.   It is easy to get gold here, but it is
very difficult to keep it.   In fact, after all, the affair is
a hazardous lottery; and those who may succeed in
getting off with their pounds of gold dust and flakes to
Europe or to the settled States, will be the few who
will win the great prizes.

In my diary, you will find a very detailed account
of our various operations and successes.   The first
place we made for was on the south bank of the Americans' River, and when the Lower or Mormon diggings,
as they are called, got over-crowded, we marched off
further up the river, which soon divides itself into two

branches, forming the North and South Forks. We reached the saw-mill, where the discovery was first made, and worked there some time; but finding inconveniences in the way, and hearing of another station, we started again. This new place is called Weber's Creek, and sometimes Rock Creek, and is a small stream running into the North Fork of the river. We being upon the southern bank of the South Fork, and Weber's Creek running into the North Fork at the north bank, we had to ford both branches of the stream to get to our new station, which we found very productive; the gold being more plentiful than in the lower diggings, and discovered in short veins, and in lumps amongst the rocks of the neighbouring ravines. We should probably not have gone any further than Weber's Creek—I sincerely wish we had not—but a good deal of fever and ague got about. The sun was terribly hot in those deep valleys all day, and the nights chill and damp. After some weeks here, then, we got restless, and set off once more, directing our course three days' journey to the north, to a place upon the Bear River, where we were led to expect not only plenty of gold, but a better temperature and a healthier climate. It was after we reached Bear Valley that our reverses began. It is utterly a savage country, where a strong arm and the rifle form the only code of laws. Up to our appearance on Bear River, we had got on with very few adventures, and considerable profit; but now came misfortunes. I shall not trouble you with them here: they are written at full length in the batch of MS. I send.

I hardly know what to do with myself here until the dry season comes round. The rains have not begun yet, but they may be expected from day to day, and then I suppose we shall have a vast influx from the interior, as it is quite impossible to camp out in the rainy season. Of course the price of any article of food and clothing will be excessive, and I almost think that the best thing for me to do, when the seamen come down, and the ships are manned again, will be to try and get a passage to the Sandwich Islands, which are not very far off, and in which it is probable that living is reasonable. I could easily get back to the mainland in time for the next dry season. What changes may take place by that time, however, I know not. The States may claim the land, and the gold within it, and send an army to enforce their rights. If so, a terrible scene of tumult and disorder may be expected. All the

lawless adventurers who are scattered about this part of
the continent are flocking down to the gold regions,
so are the Indians; and I feel pretty sure that Jona-
than will have a tough battle to fight if he wants to
keep all the bullion to himself.

I suppose that in England the people will be
pricking up their ears when they learn what we are
doing here, and that we shall have plenty of emigrants
from home. I hardly like to advise upon the subject
here; there certainly is a wonderful amount of gold.
What the chances of obtaining it and getting it taken
home may be next season, I know not. At all events,
the pursuit will be difficult in the extreme, and tolerably dangerous also.

*   *   *   *   *

Yours affectionately,

J. TYRWHITT BROOKS.

Vizetelly Brothers and Co. Printers and Engravers, Peterborough Court, 135 Fleet Street.

For EU product safety concerns, contact us at Calle de José Abascal, 56–1°,
28003 Madrid, Spain or eugpsr@cambridge.org.

www.ingramcontent.com/pod-product-compliance
Ingram Content Group UK Ltd.
Pitfield, Milton Keynes, MK11 3LW, UK
UKHW010336140625
459647UK00010B/637